Be the
Hero

More Praise for *Be the Hero*

"This book is quick, easy, and life changing, showing how it is within your power to choose how you perceive and respond to the events in your life."

—Sid Chapon, Senior Vice President/Director, Operations, People, and Culture, Leo Burnett Worldwide

"The world needs more heroes. That hero journey can best be started by absorbing the compelling messages in *Be the Hero*—a must-read book for our troubled times."

—Phil Zimbardo, PhD, author of *The Lucifer Effect*

"Noah Blumenthal uses a simple, compelling story to teach profound lessons."

—Tammy J. Winnie, Senior Director, Organization Change Management, Kellogg Company

"It has been said that how an individual deals with adversity reveals that person's true nature. *Be the Hero* will help you bring out your best, even in the worst of times."

—Warner Burke, PhD, Chair, Department of Organization and Leadership, Teachers College, Columbia University

"Blumenthal's message is powerful for all who want to make a positive difference in their lives as well as the lives of others. At Southwest Airlines, we embrace messages that support our values and mission; Blumenthal's message does this exceptionally well. This will be a tool I will recommend to my customers."

—Graham Vandergrift, Talent Management Senior Specialist, Southwest Airlines

"*Be the Hero* offers powerful lessons and reminders that each of our thoughts and actions impacts our effectiveness and our relationships with everyone around us."

—Gwyneth Meeks, Vice President, Organizational Development, MTV Networks

"Noah Blumenthal knows that the story of our life success is written one thought and one conversation at a time. In his fable *Be the Hero*, Noah has created not only a book but a user-friendly process to ensure every story we tell leads to a life of success with a very happy ending."

—Andrea T. Goeglein, PhD, host, *Books That Matter*

"Change your story, change your life! Noah Blumenthal has written a parable and reference tool that will enable you to unleash your heroism on the world. It is a life-changing read. I highly recommend it."
—**Victoria Halsey, PhD, Vice President, Applied Learning, The Ken Blanchard Companies, and coauthor of** *The Hamster Revolution*

"*Be the Hero* is more than a book; it's a compass that points the way to your better self. Blumenthal does a masterful job of making profoundly important ideas accessible and achievable, proving that you too can be the hero!"
—**Bill Treasurer, author of** *Courage Goes to Work*

"Hero or victim? It's all in the perspective. *Be the Hero* works brilliantly to enable you to see the heroic and victim stories in your own life. Noah's message to make yourself the hero is one that everyone could use."
—**Matt Langdon, founder, The Hero Construction Company**

"Our greatest heroes are firefighters, humanitarian aid workers, and leaders of nations—and coworkers, parents, and neighbors who help us survive thorny challenges of everyday life. We all know a hero when we see one. *Be the Hero* teaches us how to become one."
—**Carol Metzker, coauthor of** *Appreciative Intelligence*

"Rarely does a book come along that so effectively enables an individual to respond to life's challenges. In my thirty years of coaching, leading, and mentoring, it is unusual to find such a simple yet effective approach that can make such a significant difference in how people live their lives."
—**Ross Tartell, PhD, Adjunct Associate Professor of Psychology and Education, Teachers College, Columbia University**

"*Be the Hero* carries a simple yet powerful message that lives with you long after you finish reading it. The wisdom shared is the fundamental and foundational lesson of all wisdom traditions. Don't wait: read it now!"
—**Stewart Levine, author** *Getting to Resolution*

"Practical, enlightening, and inspiring! Noah shows us the right questions to ask for becoming heroes in our organizations and our own lives. *Be the Hero* should be on everyone's A list."
—**Marilee Adams, PhD, author of** *Change Your Questions, Change Your Life*

THREE POWERFUL WAYS
TO OVERCOME CHALLENGES
IN WORK AND LIFE

Be the
Hero

NOAH BLUMENTHAL

Foreword by Marshall Goldsmith

BK
Berrett-Koehler Publishers, Inc.
San Francisco
a BK Business book

Berrett-Koehler Publishers, Inc.
235 Montgomery Street, Suite 650
San Francisco, CA 94104-2916
Tel: (415) 288-0260   Fax: (415) 362-2512   www.bkconnection.com

Ordering Information

Quantity sales. Special discounts are available on quantity purchases by corporations, associations, and others. For details, contact the "Special Sales Department" at the Berrett-Koehler address above.
Individual sales. Berrett-Koehler publications are available through most bookstores. They can also be ordered directly from Berrett-Koehler: Tel: (800) 929-2929; Fax: (802) 864-7626; www.bkconnection.com
Orders for college textbook/course adoption use. Please contact Berrett-Koehler: Tel: (800) 929-2929; Fax: (802) 864-7626.
Orders by U.S. trade bookstores and wholesalers. Please contact Ingram Publisher Services, Tel: (800) 509-4887; Fax: (800) 838-1149; E-mail: customer.service@ ingrampublisherservices.com; or visit www.ingrampublisherservices.com/Ordering for details about electronic ordering.

Berrett-Koehler and the BK logo are registered trademarks of Berrett-Koehler Publishers, Inc.

Printed in the United States of America

Berrett-Koehler books are printed on long-lasting acid-free paper. When it is available, we choose paper that has been manufactured by environmentally responsible processes. These may include using trees grown in sustainable forests, incorporating recycled paper, minimizing chlorine in bleaching, or recycling the energy produced at the paper mill.

Library of Congress Cataloging-in-Publication Data
Blumenthal, Noah, 1972–
  Be the hero : three powerful ways to overcome challenges in work and life / Noah Blumenthal ; foreword by Marshall Goldsmith.
     p. cm.
  ISBN 978-1-60509-000-9 (hardcover : alk. paper)
  ISBN 978-1-60994-082-9 (pbk. : alk. paper)
  1. Success in business   2. Success.   3. Change (Psychology)   I. Title.

  HF5386.B573 2009
  650.1—dc22
                                2009013898
16 15 14 13 12   10 9 8 7 6 5 4 3 2 1
Design and production: Detta Penna
Copyediting: Sandra Craig
Proofreading: Judith Johnstone

To my father,
who taught me to see the world
through a hero's eyes

And my mother,
who encouraged me to act like a hero
no matter the obstacles

Contents

Foreword

~

Every once in a while a book comes along that strikes right at the core of a problem and brings a solution. We all have patterns of thinking and behavior that sabotage our effectiveness, success, and happiness. Noah Blumenthal believes that we can replace these negative patterns with a more positive approach — what he calls the way of the everyday hero. He shows that everyone can be a hero — when they choose the "right" path, even when it is difficult to do so. Around this concept, Blumenthal spins a tale that brings to life the lessons, techniques, and tools anyone can use to become an everyday hero.

This book is about changing one's perspective to become more successful. Such a change can be difficult because most of us tend to repeat behavior that is followed by positive reinforcement. If we are rewarded for being a victim, why would we ever want to change? B. F. Skinner showed that hungry pigeons would repeat meaningless twitches when the twitches, by pure chance, were followed by random small pellets of food. In much the same way, we repeat dysfunctional behavior when this behavior is followed by sympathy, money, job promotions, and so on, even if the behavior had no connection with the rewards!

So, why might we want to change? Because for most of us our deepest desire is to be happier, to be more effective, and to have peace of mind — in other words, we want to be successful.

In this great book, Noah Blumenthal shares the three secrets that will take you to success and beyond. Read it, devour it, and practice it, and you'll learn how to increase your effectiveness, improve your relationships, and find success. The benefits to you and to the people around you will be tremendous!

Marshall Goldsmith

Marshall Goldsmith is *The New York Times* best-selling author of *What Got You Here Won't Get You There*, winner of the Harold Longman Award for best business book of 2007. His new book, *Succession: Are You Ready?* is from Harvard Business Press.

Introduction:
Change Your Stories,
Change Your Life

No one is free from challenges. Work and life events stress us out, people treat us unfairly, and we sometimes feel powerless.

We have tough moments, times when we become frustrated and angry with our jobs or our lives. We may have angry bosses or customers, or we might have spouses or kids who at times feel like too much to handle. Life is uncertain, and change is constant.

When frustration settles in, we sometimes see ourselves as victims. Perhaps you can finish these victim sentences:

"My boss is a _____."
"My job _____."
"Worst of all, there's nothing I _____."

When in victim mode, people complete these sentences with words like *jerk, stinks,* and *can do*. Such statements produce a self-fulfilling mentality that makes it impossible to be your best.

Yet some people are at their best even in the toughest times. You might know some of them. No matter what happens, no matter the stress or challenge, even if they become angry or get thrown off their game, they quickly recover. And before you realize what happened, they are positive, energized, and taking productive action.

I wrote this book because I believe anyone can become that person — the person who experiences pain or doubt or tough times or unfairness but who maintains perspective, humor, and a sense of optimism. When this person faces difficult problems, he or she still performs at his or her best. This person is an everyday hero.

This book is about helping you choose to be an everyday hero.

Everyday heroes don't let life's challenges bring them down. Instead, they stay positive and find a way to overcome their obstacles. Everyday heroes don't always succeed, but they consistently act on the belief that they can do something to improve their situations and those of the people around them.

The way you think—what I call your stories—can lead you to be an everyday hero. The stories you tell can make your life positive, hopeful, and empowering or bitter, miserable, and hopeless. You can choose your response to everyday events that might disappoint, frustrate, or anger you—to react in a way that casts off the victim mentality and enables you to act with a hero's resolve.

Your stories determine your happiness and success. When you think like an everyday hero, you open the door to new possibilities. When you work in a company of heroes, communication increases, silos break down, and creative ideas multiply. You experience greater camaraderie, openness to new ideas, and receptivity to change.

Telling hero stories does more than change your state of mind. These stories lead to actions that produce:

Career success
Improved relationships
More effective conflict resolution
Increased adaptability to change
Stronger leadership
Reduced stress
Greater happiness

These outcomes arise from telling hero stories, and we can all tell hero stories. I have divided these stories into three types:

People stories. Heroes choose to feel others' pain and seek to understand their actions. Victims focus on their own pain and blame the people around them.

Situation stories. Heroes see the best in their lives and appreciate what they have. Victims focus on what is wrong in their lives.

Self stories. Heroes believe they can influence their lives and choose to take action. Victims believe nothing can be done to improve their lives.

No one tells hero stories all the time. We all lapse into victim mentality occasionally. Part of being an everyday hero is recognizing those lapses and shifting back to hero stories.

The techniques and strategies presented in this book come out of my years of corporate coaching and consulting, helping everyone from senior executives to line workers to entrepreneurs achieve greater success and peace of mind at the same time. These strategies also come from my personal experiences as an employee, manager, business owner, husband, and father.

In the last decade, first as a founding member of an internal consulting group at a Fortune 500 company, then as the founder and president of my own consulting company, I have coached hundreds of corporate executives facing work crises, family challenges, life decisions, and moral dilemmas. I have taught thousands of people how to accept accountability and lead themselves to the life and work experiences they desire.

Each time I explore a story with one of my clients, we both learn from the experience. I am grateful to all of my clients for helping me understand the power of our stories. Each time I catch myself in a victim story, I also learn. The lessons from all of these experiences are captured in this book.

To support you in shifting your stories, the book is divided into two parts: a parable and a resource guide.

Parable

In the parable we follow the story of Jeff, a good guy with talent and high hopes whose life throws him some unexpected challenges. His struggle is one I believe we have all faced. How do you respond positively to adversity without letting it bring you down? With a little help, he discovers the answer, and so will you.

I wrote this book as a parable because I think the story brings the lessons to life and makes them easier and more fun to digest. Although this story is fictional, the characters draw from many people in my life — my family, friends, colleagues, clients, and of course myself.

However, one part of this parable is true. That story has been one of the greatest inspirations of my life. If you can't guess which part that is while you read the parable, you'll find out in the afterword.

Resource Guide

The lessons of the parable will be evident, but that doesn't mean they will automatically translate into sustained behavior change. Therefore, a resource guide after the parable offers specific tips and tools you can use to carry the lessons from this book into your work and life.

I have done my best to provide effective lessons in this book. However, changing your stories is a skill that takes practice over time. I still discover more every day. In order for me to share these lessons, www.be-the-hero.com features a reader's section that will be updated with more information and tools to help individuals and managers succeed.

You will also have access to a forum where you can connect with others who are seeking to live and work like heroes, and you will be able to ask me questions about the heroic challenges in your work and life. Your access code to enter the reader's section of the Web site can be found in the resource guide of this book.

I hope you enjoy this book, and I invite you to be the hero you want to be.

Noah Blumenthal
July 2009

Parable

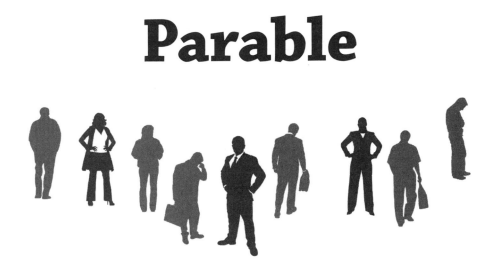

Challenges of Work and Life

The Funk

Jeff was in a rut.

The day started off with a familiar pattern. His alarm rang and he hit the snooze button. He used to wake up on the first ring. Today it took him four snoozes.

"Why is this happening to me?" This wasn't the first time he had asked himself the question. It had become a common lament, usually followed by, "When is my life going to get better?"

Jeff's company had recently adopted the acronym B-HAG, which stood for Big Hairy Audacious Goal. B-HAGs were supposed to energize people and encourage them to strive for greater things. Jeff had adjusted the term slightly. By the time he cut himself shaving and spilled his coffee, Jeff had declared the day a B-HAD. For him B-HAD stood for Big Hairy Atrocious Day, and lately he felt almost every day was a B-HAD.

Jeff had never experienced a funk like this in his life, and it was quite possible things were about to get worse. Today he had to hand in his year-end performance appraisal to Yvette, his boss.

Jeff wasn't certain how Yvette would rate him, but he was willing to bet she would not have good news. She had been on his case constantly lately. He knew he had to be on his best behavior, but all he wanted to do was tell her to shove this job. Each day he felt like he was about to lose his cool completely and do more than a few things he would certainly regret.

Everything in his life was going south. His relationship with Yvette had been deteriorating for months. His nine-month-old daughter, Siena, had colic, which he was convinced was a medical term that meant the doctors had given up trying to figure out why she cried twenty-four hours a day. The lack of sleep and the baby's continuous crying put a major strain on his relationship with Marie, his wife.

In the past when he got frustrated he used to play basketball or go for a bike ride or a long walk. These days he always had reasons to stay late at work, and if he actually did get home at a reasonable time, he had to help out with Siena. Forget about taking time or doing anything for himself. Those days were long gone, and his stress was mounting.

Given that he had to hand in his performance appraisal, Jeff was anticipating the worst from this day. Just a few hours later it would shock him to discover he felt happier than he could remember feeling in months.

The Good Life

Life hadn't always been so challenging. Everything used to fall into place for Jeff. In fact, even now most of Jeff's friends and colleagues thought he was successful and fortunate. There were no speed bumps, tragedies, or meltdowns. Jeff's best friend, Art, had nicknamed him Smooth because everything in his life seemed to flow.

Art's life was anything but smooth. His parents divorced when he was ten, and while Art was in college his father died from cancer. Every time Art dated a new woman he seemed to go through a cycle of euphoria, disappointment, and boredom. Art had sold furniture, paper, pharmaceuticals, and financial services. He seemed to need to find a new job each time he bought a new pair of shoes. When the shoes wore out, the job had to go.

Jeff's life looked nothing like that. He had an intelligent, beautiful wife with a great sense of humor. Most of his friends had joked that he definitely married up. Jeff agreed. He was one of the youngest people in his company to get promoted to a management position. He had a daughter who, aside from crying all the time, was healthy. So why didn't things feel great on the inside?

Jeff used to think of himself as lucky. It wasn't that he got everything he wanted, but starting early in his life, things seemed to work out well for him.

When he tried out for his high school basketball team, he wasn't the star player, but he made the team and performed well. When his friends were stressing out over getting into college, he was accepted early to the college of his choice. He had always been viewed as a leader and was well liked by other students and by the parents, teachers, and professors he had come to know in his youth.

Then he graduated from college and got a job, but before he started his new job, Jeff and Art headed to Europe for three weeks of fun. With a travel guide that promised they would see Europe for under $50 per day, they left in search of unforgettable experiences.

They went to the running of the bulls in Pamplona and the opera in Prague. They dined on escargot in Paris and wurst in Berlin. They saw the Roman Coliseum and the Palace of Versailles. They traveled through seven countries in three weeks, but one experience always stood out for Jeff.

The Guru

Toward the end of their trip, Jeff and Art landed in the small Swiss town of Interlaken, which is surrounded by some of the most beautiful mountain peaks a traveler can find.

When they arrived at the youth hostel, they dumped their backpacks in their room and headed to the common area where travelers gathered to share food, drinks, and stories.

Jeff looked around and saw the usual mix of happy, bedraggled youths, but his eye was caught by a bulletin board covered with pictures on one of the walls. Most of the pictures were of people standing on top of a mountain smiling, but something else made their expressions noteworthy — something in their eyes, some kind of knowing look.

"What do you see?"

The question took Jeff by surprise. He turned around to discover that an old man with a long beard had asked the question. Beyond the old man, Jeff was not surprised to see Art sitting at a table with two women, talking animatedly and pointing in Jeff's direction.

Jeff turned back to the man and said, "They seem happy."

He was about to leave and catch up with Art, but before he moved the old man asked him, "Is that all you see? The people in the pictures seem happy?"

Jeff thought momentarily about whether or not to share his observations with this stranger, but then he figured why not? Interesting conversations were kind of the point of these places.

"At first that was what I noticed, but if you look closer, it isn't just happiness. They all seem like they know a secret. That probably sounds dumb. I mean, how can a smile tell you someone knows a secret?"

"No, it's not dumb, but I agree their smiles don't tell you that. It's in their eyes."

Jeff felt a surge of excitement hearing his own thoughts spoken by the man. "That's right! It *is* in their eyes. They look like they're seeing more than just the camera."

"In a way they are. They're looking at the world in a brand new way." The old man gestured to an empty table and sat down. Without thinking, Jeff sat down with him.

"Kids come here all the time looking to do some sightseeing and meet other travelers. They leave here with a few memories, but some leave here with more."

Jeff thought the man was being a little melodramatic, but he was intrigued all the same and asked him what he meant.

"The mountains are the reason people visit Interlaken. Everyone sees beautiful views. However, some see something far more precious."

For the first time Jeff looked deep into the man's eyes. He could see then that this man had the same look as the people in the photos. He knew the secret.

The old man continued, "When you are surrounded by the kind of beauty you will see on these mountains, it can be overwhelming. It can make macho guys like you want to cry it is so beautiful. Most people rebel against those feelings. They don't want to let themselves be exposed to such powerful forces. They are afraid of what they will feel or see or know. So they don't let themselves slow down and deeply experience the moment. They take out their cameras, snap a few photos, and then head back down the mountain as quickly as they can. They may have seen the beauty around them, but they didn't absorb it in a way that would change them forever."

At this point Jeff started to feel a little uneasy. Part of him believed what the man was saying and was afraid he would be one of the ones who would rush past the experience. Part of him doubted this man and was afraid he was being made a fool by listening to this story. When he looked at the man's eyes, though, that part disappeared. He could see the knowledge in this man's eyes, and he wanted to know what the hikers in the photos knew.

"What about the ones who aren't afraid of the experience," asked Jeff. "What happens to them?"

"Well," said the man, "most of them are afraid, too, but they don't let that stop them. They stand there on the mountain and they drink it in. They look at the scenery, but they also look at themselves. They feel the weight of these enormous mountains and the awesome power that created such marvels. These hikers who drink up the experience feel their own frailty and the mistakes of their past. They also feel their own strength, their triumphs. Then something shifts in their perspective. They see themselves and the world in a whole new way, a way that changes everything."

Jeff furrowed his brow in confusion. "How do they do that?"

Before the old man could answer, Jeff felt a hand on his shoulder. He turned to see Art looking down at him with a big grin on his face.

"We're all set for tomorrow. I have the day planned out, and we've got company, too."

Usually Jeff would have been eager for whatever Art had planned, but right now he wanted to have the experience the old man had described. He wanted to know what he meant about a perspective that changed everything. He turned back to ask the old man to explain, but he was gone — heading toward a door at the back of the common room.

Jeff thought momentarily about chasing after him, but the old man had said what he had to say and moved on. Jeff turned back to Art, frustrated but resigned that he might not learn the secret of the mountaintop.

"OK, what's the plan?"

"Well, the women I met got a hiking map and recommendations from the Guru and said we should all go together in their car."

Jeff gave him a confused look. "Who's the Guru?"

Now Art looked confused. "He's the guy you've been sitting here talking to for the last twenty minutes. He runs this place. They said everyone calls him the Guru."

At that moment Jeff realized he had never asked the man's name. He didn't know anything about him, but he suddenly felt very excited to see what he would discover on his hike tomorrow.

The Hike

Jeff and Art left early the next morning with their new friends, Suzanne and Alexa, and as predicted, the scenery was spectacular. The pine forests were rugged. The peaks above showed jagged rocks and snowcaps. Jeff found himself wondering if it could get any better higher up on the mountain. He would soon discover it could.

They found the trailhead the Guru had recommended and began their hike. Before they reached any of the great views from the top of the trail, they had a lot of climbing to do. Art happily sparked up conversations along the way.

Art relived old memories of high school with Jeff. They talked about what was waiting for them when they returned from their trip, a job for Jeff, uncertainty for Art, who had yet to find a job. Jeff went along with the conversation, though he was pretty sure this wasn't what the Guru had in mind when he talked about finding a new perspective.

So Jeff was happy when Art moved on to start a conversation with Alexa, and Suzanne naturally fell in step with him. Suzanne seemed to be soaking up the atmosphere, and Jeff was content to remain silent as they hiked farther up the mountain.

Now and then they stopped when the terrain broke up to allow them a broader view of the surrounding mountains. Each time they stopped, Jeff felt a greater sense of awe about their surroundings. When he thought he might be nearing the experience the Guru had described, he wanted to confirm it.

He turned to Suzanne and said, "So you and Alexa spoke to the Guru, too?"

Alexa and Art were about fifty yards up the trail. The faint sound of giggling drifted down from where they walked.

"No," Suzanne replied. "Alexa wasn't there. I spoke to the Guru alone."

Jeff wondered if her experience with the Guru was similar to his. He asked, "What did you talk about with him?"

Suzanne gazed off at the terrain and said, "It was kind of a weird conversation — hard to explain."

Jeff had to know if her conversation was like his. "Was it about this hike and the way you see the world?"

Suzanne looked a little surprised, then she smiled. "Yes, it was."

"Mine, too," Jeff said.

They both gazed into the distance, feeling a sense of peace and kinship with one another before they returned to silently climbing.

It took about four hours to reach the top of the trail: a clearing above the tree line in a spot where the mountain seemed to fade out of the way to allow unobstructed views in almost every direction.

Jeff wanted to absorb the whole scene, but it was too much. He couldn't look in every direction at once, and every time he turned his head he felt as if he were seeing something even more spectacular. Now Jeff understood what the Guru meant — just looking at the scenery could be overwhelming.

Having started early, they arrived at the top with plenty of time to eat and soak up the views. As they rested and stretched their muscles, Jeff noticed Art and Alexa were carrying on a continuous conversation. They weren't spending much time looking around.

He remembered what the Guru said: some people want to get off the mountain to escape the gravity of the experience. Art and Alexa appeared to be running away without running off the mountain. Their conversation seemed like their way to avoid the deep feelings created by this place.

When he looked at Suzanne, he saw something quite different, and he could tell she didn't want to talk. She just sat quietly, gazing into the distance. Now and then she would shift her view. She looked peaceful. Jeff thought he and Suzanne were clearly having a deeper experience than Art and Alexa.

Looking at the scenery, Jeff thought about his past and his future. He thought about his mistakes and his successes and about what the secret might be that he was supposed to discover on this mountain. What kept coming to mind was that climbing this mountain was a triumphant experience. He wanted to hold onto that.

So he made a decision about how he would view the world. He decided he would hold onto the feeling he had of being on top of the world. He would live like he was always on top of the mountain.

Upon coming to this conclusion, Jeff stood up to stretch his legs. As he walked around, his feet practically bounced off the mountainside, feeling lighter than air. A grin spread across Jeff's face as he imagined a phenomenal life unfolding before him.

Then the others stood up, took lots of pictures, and they all hiked down the mountain. Jeff thought this day would be memorable because he changed the way he viewed the world. He was wrong.

Three days after Jeff and Art returned home, Jeff reviewed their pictures from the trip. They had a lot of pictures from their three weeks in Europe, but the one that stood out for Jeff was the picture of the four of them on top of the mountain.

They all looked happy in that picture, but two of them had a special look in their eyes. Two of them looked as though they knew a secret. What surprised Jeff was that those two people were Suzanne and Art.

It would be almost a decade before Jeff discovered why.

The Fast Track

It was easy for Jeff to put away his concerns about the picture from the top of the mountain. Only a few days after viewing the vacation photos, Jeff started his new job and quickly convinced himself he was living like he was on top of the mountain.

His company operated at a fast pace that Jeff loved, and he threw himself into his work. As was the pattern in his life, he may not have been the best new hire in the company, but he did distinguish himself.

At the end of his second year he was put in the company's Fast Track program, where he spent three years rotating through all the different areas of the company. For four months at a time, he worked in various offices and functions for different people and on different projects, learning more than he thought his brain could hold.

The assignments were both exhausting and invigorating, which is how Jeff would have described his personal life as well. During his Fast Track years he met Marie, the woman of his dreams. She was a musician who easily switched between cello and piano, but her most amazing quality was her ability to laugh. It was her laugh that made Jeff fall in love.

At about the same time as the Fast Track ended, Jeff and Marie married. At work he received a permanent assignment working in the marketing department, and at home he got a permanent partner to share his ups and downs.

In the marketing department Jeff loved the combination of analytical and creative work. Once again he threw himself into his work, with a fair degree of success. His manager decided to reward him by volunteering him for a cross-functional team that was looking at cost-saving ideas for the company.

Again his work and his personal life seemed to be in sync. Only the week before this new opportunity arose, Marie had told Jeff she was pregnant. Life seemed just about perfect.

The cross-functional team's project was challenging and long. During the many months they worked together, Jeff made a strong impression on one of the other team members.

Yvette was an executive in the company, and before he knew it, she had offered him a management position in her department.

It seemed like the chance of a lifetime.

Jeff was sitting in Yvette's office, and she was actually trying to convince him to take her job offer. Jeff just listened. Did she really think he wasn't already sold? Wouldn't he have to be crazy not to jump at this? It was all he could do to keep an ear-to-ear grin off his face.

"I know you haven't been in your job very long," Yvette said, "but I think this is exactly the kind of stretch assignment that would be great for you. You're better off moving to a new job before you get too comfortable with your current one. I've always said I'd rather be busy than bored, and I know this position will keep you busy with new and exciting work."

She went on to explain that Jeff would grow into the position. He was smart and picked things up quickly. There would be a steep learning curve, but she had confidence in him.

"I watched the way you interacted with other team members on the cost-saving project, and I think you will be a natural as a manager."

Hearing this praise was an odd experience for Jeff. His pride exulted that an executive in the company should see him so positively. At the same time, his fears ran rampant. Was he as good as she thought? Could he live up to her expectations? In the end his pride won.

As Yvette went on, Jeff imagined himself as a manager. He saw himself as the team captain, the fearless leader. He dreamed of his team charging through walls for him.

"Just in case you aren't convinced," Yvette continued, "I'll point out the obvious benefits. You'll be jumping to a new pay grade, and the last three people I hired into management positions got further promotions within twenty-four months. I don't need you to make a decision today. I just need to know if you are interested so I can move the process forward and formalize the financial offer. So what do you think?"

Jeff was dumbfounded. What did he think? He thought he couldn't believe he was getting this kind of opportunity. He thought he couldn't understand why she wanted him for this position. He thought he would gladly take this position even if it came with a decrease in salary.

He was pretty sure he didn't mask his glee very well as a grin crept across his face, nearly connecting his ears to one another. However, he felt good about himself for having enough composure to simply say, "Thank you for your interest in me. I'd be very happy to see what the offer would be for this position."

As he left her office, Jeff felt he was once again living life as if he were on top of the mountain. Four weeks later, he had accepted the new job and was working for Yvette. He had a team of six people working for him, and he had a lot to learn.

He was ready for the challenge. What he wasn't ready for was wondering if accepting the position had been a huge mistake.

Falling Down

Jeff was on the fast track and had just been promoted. Then his child arrived. He and Marie named her Siena, and immediately he understood what the phrase "Daddy's little girl" meant. From the moment he first saw her, he knew he would do anything for her. But things weren't perfect for long.

People talked about the ways parenthood would change things, but nothing had prepared Jeff for this. He had heard it all from friends and family members — the crying, the diapers, the sleepless nights — but how do you describe sleep deprivation to someone who had never experienced it? Although people had warned him, he had never truly understood how difficult it would be, and Siena wasn't making it any easier.

None of this made Jeff perform at his best at work. Then, at about the time Marie went back to work, Jeff's work situation started to turn sour.

He had been in his new job for about three months and he was still getting to know the players on his team. Still, he knew enough to recognize Sarah was his top performer. When she came into his office to hand in her resignation, his heart sank. Not only was she leaving, but she was going to their chief competitor. When Jeff went to tell Yvette the news, he didn't expect her to be happy.

It was the end of the day on a Friday, and when he got to her office, Jeff found Yvette pouring her usual late-afternoon mug of coffee, the third of her daily ritual coffee drinks. Yvette operated at a breakneck pace most of the day. Her coffee times were when she slowed down, when she shifted out of rapid-fire decision mode and into a more contemplative, reflective frame of mind.

Yvette's coffee routine was one of the quirks Jeff had become accustomed to. She considered herself more than a coffee addict — she was obsessed. She kept a coffeemaker in her office, and she used only top-quality beans, which of course she ground herself.

Jeff hated to interrupt this ritual, but Yvette had already seen him. She was now looking over at him as she inhaled the aroma of her coffee.

I might as well get it over with, he thought.

"Hi, Yvette," he said as he walked in and sat down in one of the chairs opposite her desk.

"Hi, Jeff. Coffee?" She always asked. That, too, was part of her ritual.

"No, thanks," he responded, as always. He figured he might someday catch the coffee bug, but it hadn't happened to him yet. "I have something I need to tell you."

Yvette raised her eyebrows. "For some reason I've never heard good news follow that statement. What's up?"

Jeff shared the news about Sarah and could immediately see the disappointment in Yvette's face. Whatever calm she attained while sniffing her coffee had disappeared in an instant.

"OK," Yvette said. "Let's explore."

This was one of her pet phrases. Yvette loved to poke around and discover. The truth was her questions always impressed Jeff when she went into exploration mode, but today he felt a little nervous. He felt that losing Sarah was a big deal, and he honestly didn't know what to do about it. Yvette's disappointment seemed already clear on her face.

"What do we know?" That was her usual opening question.

"Well, we know she is our top performer. She came to the company two years ago and has consistently distinguished herself. My predecessor gave her a glowing review when I took over as manager, and I have seen her continue to perform exceptionally."

"What did she like about her job?"

Jeff hesitated a little. He wasn't sure what Yvette wanted to hear, and truth be told, he didn't know Sarah that well.

"I think she liked the work itself. She was very good at her job. So she must have gotten a sense of accomplishment."

"OK. What didn't she like about her job?"

Now Jeff hesitated even longer. What was running through his mind was that she stayed in her job and was happy for almost two years. The only thing that had changed was she got a new manager, but he didn't want to say he was the reason for her departure.

"I don't really know," Jeff answered lamely. He knew it was a lousy response, but he was afraid to reveal his true thoughts.

"OK, first key lesson: always know what people don't like about their jobs. If you don't know the answer, you can't improve their situation. One of your jobs as a manager is to ask people what they don't like."

Yvette always included key lessons as part of her exploration process. Usually Jeff didn't mind and even looked forward to hearing the lessons. He wanted to learn, but today he was feeling insecure over Sarah's departure. His anxiety made him defensive.

Suddenly, instead of thinking Yvette had made a good point, Jeff thought of her as a hypocrite. After all, she had never asked him what he didn't like. If that was such a key lesson, why wasn't she following her own advice?

Yvette continued to explore with more questions and more lessons, but Jeff wasn't listening today the way he usually did. He was frustrated and disappointed in himself, and he grew annoyed with Yvette. Fortunately, she didn't seem to notice his reaction. After a while she wished him a good weekend and told him to come back fired up on Monday.

Unfortunately, the following week things didn't get much better. One of Yvette's peers pointed out a big mistake in a report Jeff's team had prepared. When Yvette took Jeff exploring, he was in no mood for her key lessons.

The week after that one of their important clients, Amanda Kim, called to complain. Lee, one of Jeff's team members, had promised to send Amanda some information and had forgotten. The complaint arrived on a day when Jeff and Lee were traveling to see another client. So when Amanda couldn't speak to Lee and then asked to speak to a manager, her call was forwarded to Yvette.

When Jeff returned from his trip, he felt ambushed. There was an angry message from Amanda and a note from Yvette to come see her in her office. He could already imagine the scene that would play out — going through explorations and lessons to point out more and more ways he was deficient in his new role.

First, he called Amanda. She was angry and said she hoped he would find a way to improve his team's reliability. He apologized and, as Yvette had already done, promised her he would send her the information by the following day.

One unpleasant task done, it was time for the second one.

He went to Yvette's office and knocked on the door. As expected, she wanted to talk about Amanda and his lessons learned. Jeff talked and listened and tried not to let his frustration show. The conversation went pretty much as he expected, with one surprise.

After what Jeff felt was beating the Amanda situation to death, Yvette changed the subject. She said she wasn't going to be able to spend as much time with him going forward. She had just been assigned to another cross-functional team for a very important strategic initiative of the company. It was going to take a lot of her time. So she expected Jeff to be more independent.

It was all he could do not to grin. Receiving less attention from Yvette seemed like the best news he could get right at that moment.

"I'll do my best to figure things out on my own and respect your time," he said.

"I know you will. You always do. And don't forget. If you run into trouble, just go exploring. The key lessons will show up if you just ask some good questions."

Jeff left her office wondering why she had to be so pushy with her annoying exploring, but he had a smile on his face. Less time with Yvette was exactly what the doctor ordered.

For the next three months Jeff was able to operate with a great deal of independence. He even found himself going exploring on a few occasions, but his life was still dominated by exhaustion.

The truth was Siena was getting better at sleeping at night, but she wasn't getting better fast enough for Jeff. He and Marie were fighting a lot over what to do.

Jeff wanted to try anything to get Siena to sleep through the night, up to and including letting her cry it out all night long if that's what it would take. Marie hated the idea of letting Siena cry. She had been reading book after book about what you could do, looking for what she considered "humane" methods. Unfortunately, Siena wasn't going for these. Now Jeff wanted to let her cry, and Marie couldn't accept that.

Then Yvette's task force completed its mission, and Jeff felt his freedom come to an end. Almost immediately she was back on his case. One of her peers had observed that Jeff appeared unhappy. Yvette told him that wasn't the kind of impression Jeff wanted to make with people. To stay on the fast track, he needed people to see him as positive and upbeat.

Jeff wanted to scream, "How in the world are you supposed to be upbeat on six months of three hours of sleep per night? I do my job. I work hard. What more do you want from me? Why don't you just leave me alone?"

When he left Yvette's office, he knew his lack of sleep was getting to him in a big way. The months continued to pass by in an exhausted haze. To Jeff, his life was a blur of sleepless nights and frustrating days with no end in sight.

The Team Meeting

It was getting close to the end of the year. Jeff decided to hold a planning meeting with his team. He emailed everyone that he wanted to discuss their goals for the following year, and he encouraged them to come to the meeting with any ideas they had for new directions for themselves or the group. He thought he was doing the right thing—being a good manager and leader.

Somehow Yvette got wind of the meeting and asked Jeff if she could attend. It wasn't the kind of request Jeff thought he could refuse. When the day of the meeting came, Jeff felt ready. He had prepared a solid agenda and had lots of ideas to share. If Yvette was going to judge him today, he would show her that hiring him had been a great decision.

At ten o'clock Jeff walked into the conference room. Half his team was already there, and the rest quickly filed in. Yvette wasn't there yet, but Jeff decided not to wait. She was usually on time, so if she hadn't shown up yet it was possible she had to cancel.

That's just fine by me, Jeff thought.

He kicked off the meeting by asking the team to brainstorm their biggest successes of the year. There was a lot of energy around this conversation. People were excited as they recounted accolades they had received from their clients and senior management. Jeff felt like the meeting was off to a great start.

Next he asked the team to brainstorm their biggest disappointments. Jeff was in the middle of writing DISAPPOINT-MENTS at the top of a flip chart when Yvette walked into the conference room.

The first thought to race through Jeff's mind was, "That's just perfect. Of course she missed the success discussion."

"Sorry I'm late, everyone." Yvette said. "Please don't stop for me. Just keep going with your discussion."

Jeff could feel the room tense up, but he had to continue. "All right, everyone, it's less fun to talk about, but let's bring the same energy to this discussion that we had when we talked about our successes."

Slowly a few ideas came up, but it was like pulling teeth. Jeff was frustrated by the reluctance in the room, and his frustration only increased when he saw the look of consternation on Yvette's face. After glancing her way he pushed even harder.

"Wendy, Julian, what about some of the challenges you experienced working with the national sales desk at the beginning of the year? Do you want to talk about those experiences?"

The two Jeff had singled out exchanged a long look. Then Wendy turned to Jeff and said, "That was a frustrating situation. We did a lot of work on the 5 IN 5 growth campaign. Then we asked national sales to partner with us in introducing it to the sales force. Before we knew what was happening, they were presenting it as their idea and taking all the credit."

Here Julian jumped in. "Yeah. The salespeople and the executives here in the home office all seemed to heap the praise on them without recognizing us at all."

"I remember how frustrated you were," Jeff replied. "Most of that happened right before I came on board. I wish I had been here earlier so someone could have supported you when you needed it."

As soon as the words were out of his mouth, Jeff realized they were a mistake. Yvette had been overseeing the group right before he arrived. His statement pointed the finger at her. He glanced her way, but her expression hadn't changed. Maybe she hadn't made the connection.

In any case, Jeff decided it was time to move on. He also decided it was time for him to prove his value to Yvette.

"Now let's talk about the future. I want everyone to give me one goal or new project or idea you think we should consider for next year. Nothing is off limits."

Julian, who was sitting directly across the table from Jeff, spoke first. "I think we should create some kind of follow-up to the 5 IN 5 campaign. Maybe 4 MORE 4 SURE."

He pronounced the last word "shore," and there were some groans around the table and some good-natured ribbing over the rhyme. Someone mentioned the words "kindergarten concept," but it was all in jest. Jeff felt the mood was positive, and he actually saw Yvette nodding her head with half a smile.

"Who's next?" asked Jeff.

Tyson was sitting next to Julian and threw out an idea. "I think we should expand our newsletter. I was thinking about doing monthly case studies and maybe some kind of instant poll."

"Great," said Jeff. "Let's get everyone's ideas out and then we can talk specifics."

Next came Kim, who was sitting to Tyson's left, and the pattern was established that they were going around the table in order. When it came around to Jeff he glanced at Yvette. She seemed in good spirits, and he figured he would never have a better chance.

"I have something to propose that is a little different." Jeff took a deep breath and launched into his vision for the coming year. He had thought a lot about this and had details and arguments to back up every piece of his plan. If this didn't wow Yvette, he didn't know what would.

He covered nearly every aspect of the team. Each time he touched on responsibilities or tasks specific to certain team members, he made sure to ask them for input, but everyone seemed in agreement with what he was proposing. The farther along he went, the more he picked up steam. Before Jeff knew it, Tyson raised his hand and apologized for having to leave the meeting. It was noon and he had a lunch meeting with a client.

Jeff hadn't realized how much time had passed. "This is a good time to adjourn the meeting anyway. Let's plan another all-hands meeting next week and pick up with this topic."

Everyone cleared out of the room until Jeff and Yvette were the only ones left. He was eager to hear her reaction to his plan and was completely unprepared for what she would tell him.

Blindsided

Jeff walked over to where Yvette was sitting and leaned against the table, eager to hear her take on his performance.

"Tell me what you thought of the meeting," Yvette said.

"I thought it went well. You missed the beginning when we had a great conversation about our successes from this year. Then we got some really good ideas on the table for next year."

"Tell me. What were the good ideas?" Yvette asked.

"Well, we've been talking about them for the last hour or so. Which ones do you want to discuss?"

Yvette suddenly looked very tired. "I don't really want to discuss any of them. It's not that the ideas aren't worth discussing. It's that I don't think you realize what happened just now."

Jeff could feel the rug being pulled out from under him. He didn't know what Yvette was going to say next, but he recognized the sinking feeling in his stomach.

"What does that mean?" he said. "What do you think happened?" Jeff realized his voice was rising, but he couldn't control it.

"Jeff, you have great enthusiasm, but it hurt you today. You were so eager to talk about your own ideas you didn't listen to or consider anyone else's. The last ninety minutes of that meeting consisted of you telling everyone what they were going to do next year."

"Wait a second. That's not fair." Jeff's anger was beginning to come through in his tone. "Everyone loved the ideas. I checked in with every single team member. They all agreed." Jeff could feel his frustration building. She was always on his case.

"Jeff, no one contradicted you, but no one supported you either." Now Yvette's voice was rising to match his. "You were pushing your ideas in front of your manager. Of course no one stood up to tell you they disagreed. I'd be willing to bet no one here bought in either. You talked almost nonstop for an hour and a half. You didn't create any real dialogue."

Jeff was struggling to keep himself under control. "What are you talking about? I brought great ideas here today. Now the ideas are no good because I talked about them?"

"Jeff, what do you think is going on here? I'm on your side." Suddenly Yvette shook her head and gathered up her things. "When you are ready to talk about this calmly, let me know."

With that she walked out of the conference room. Jeff was left standing there, wondering what had gone so wrong. How could they have judged the meeting so differently?

It felt as though Yvette had it in for him. He was aggravated and exhausted, and he just wanted to find some way to regain his footing. He remembered he once had a positive relationship with Yvette. In fact, he remembered he once thought life would always feel as if he were on top of a mountain. If only there was some way to regain that feeling.

People Stories

An Old Friend

It was the Monday after the meeting, and Jeff was staring at his year-end self-appraisal form wondering what he could possibly write. He hadn't crossed paths with Yvette since the meeting, and now he had no idea where he stood with her. Every time he looked at the appraisal form his mind drifted to his worst moments with Yvette. He shook his head, trying to remove the negative images, to no avail.

"I have to get out of here," Jeff said aloud. He looked up quickly to see if anyone was walking by and might have overheard him talking to himself. No one was in the hallway.

Jeff got up and walked out of his office. He took the elevator to the lobby, which opened up into a large, bright atrium. Jeff headed over to the side that housed a coffee shop. The breakfast rush was over, and very few people were around. Jeff walked over to the refrigerator and grabbed a bottle of apple juice. As always, since he didn't drink coffee, he felt like the odd one out buying juice at the coffee shop.

After paying for his drink, he walked back into the atrium and looked up at the sky through the ceiling of windows, not really sure what to do or where to go. He had left his office to calm down, stop thinking, try to relax, but he couldn't. His mind kept snapping back to his performance review and his anger toward Yvette.

Suddenly realizing that he had been standing in the same spot in the middle of the floor for who knows how long, Jeff quickly glanced around to see if anyone was watching him. In fact, he discovered a very tall man was looking at him and walking in his direction. A little embarrassed, Jeff started to turn and walk away. Then something about the man registered in the back of Jeff's mind.

He took another look and broke into a wide grin as he realized who it was.

The man walked up to Jeff and said, "You're still wearing the same goofy grin on your face."

Jeff, not to be outdone, replied, "And is it possible you've gotten even lankier?"

The man laughed out loud, then clasped hands with Jeff and gave him a bear hug. His name was Martin, and he had been a senior and the starting center on Jeff's high school basketball team when Jeff first came on as a freshman.

Martin sized Jeff up and said, "It's good to see you, though it's hard for me to get my mind around the idea of you being all grown up and looking so professional."

As if he were back in high school, Jeff wanted to keep up with Martin. "Right back at you," he said lamely.

For the next ten minutes Jeff completely forgot about his troubles at home and at work as he easily slid back into youthful banter with his old friend. They reviewed who each of them was still in touch with from the team, rehashing stories about each person as they went.

Then Martin asked Jeff what he was up to these days, and all of the weight of his troubles came back to him in an instant.

"These days I feel like my job is to pull my hair out."

The comment was out of his mouth before he even realized what he was saying. It surprised him that he had spoken so openly, but Martin had always been the guy everyone wanted to have as a friend. When you had a problem with a girlfriend, you went to Martin. When you needed to know how to deal with a particular teacher, Martin was your man.

"I'm sorry to hear that," Martin responded. "What's your story that has you feeling so upset?"

When Jeff looked at Martin his anger turned to surprise. He saw a look in Martin's eyes that reminded him of the vacation photos from his postcollege journey. Martin had the same knowing look as the people on the bulletin board in the youth hostel, the same look Suzanne and Art had on top of the mountain. Jeff thought about living like he was on top of the mountain, and he knew it had been a long time since he had felt like he lived that way. Still, he wasn't quite ready to spill his guts in the middle of the atrium.

"It's nothing—just life."

Martin glanced at his watch. "Well, unfortunately, I have to run to a meeting, but I'm interested to hear about that life of yours. Maybe I can even help you stop pulling out your hair. Are you free for lunch today? I'd be happy to catch up some more and talk to you about your story."

Jeff said he was available, and they agreed to meet at noon. Before leaving one another they exchanged business cards.

"Martin," Jeff said, "is this for real?"

"What?"

"Your card says your title is hero coach. What is that supposed to mean?"

Martin smiled. "I'll see you at lunch and tell you all about it."

With that, Martin crossed the lobby and disappeared into the elevator. Jeff again looked down at the card he had received. It still read the same. Martin's company was called Hero's Perspective, and his title was hero coach.

Jeff wasn't looking forward to going back to his office, but now he was very curious about what he would learn at lunch.

Three Types of Stories

Jeff rushed through his morning schedule and tried to get a jump on the work he had planned for the afternoon. He wanted to have a clear calendar for his lunch with Martin.

Then, closer to noon, Jeff began to have second thoughts. He looked at the picture of Marie and Siena on his desk, and a part of him wanted to skip this lunch. Things had been pretty lousy for him lately. Did he really want to sit down with Martin and talk about how his life was falling apart?

Martin always had it together. It was no surprise that he was successful. He probably had the perfect family to go along with his career as a Hero Coach, whatever that was.

Still, he didn't want to stand up his old friend. So a few minutes before noon, he found himself for the second time that day standing in the lobby, not fully knowing why he was there.

Jeff must have been daydreaming because Martin was standing right in front of him before he realized it.

"You ready?" Martin asked.

Jeff nodded and Martin led the way out of the building.

Martin set a brisk pace as they wove around the other pedestrians, so they didn't talk on the way to the restaurant. Martin's choice turned out to be an Italian restaurant a handful of blocks away.

"I've never been here before," Jeff said.

"Best place around," Martin replied with a grin. "I made a reservation. Let me see if our table is ready."

The long line of customers suggested Martin might be right about the quality of the restaurant. While Martin walked up to the host stand, Jeff soaked up the atmosphere. He watched the chefs in the open kitchen tossing pizza dough in the air, sautéing vegetables, and working the grill.

When he looked back to the host desk, he saw Martin in what appeared to be a very serious conversation with the host. He thought their reservation must have been lost, but then Martin waved him over as the host led them to a comfortable booth with a view of the kitchen.

As Jeff sat, the host gave him a smile and handed him an open menu. There were plenty of standard Italian offerings, but clearly this place specialized in gourmet pizza. The many varieties had toppings and flavors ranging from Indian to Greek to Moroccan.

When the host returned, Martin ordered the Smiling Sal pizza: grilled chicken, spinach, walnuts, sauce, gouda, and mozzarella.

Jeff breathed in deeply and savored the aromas wafting around the room. Then he ordered a Lucca Bene pizza: prosciutto, porcini mushrooms, mozzarella, and tomatoes.

The host gave him a wink. "You're going to like that a lot. Your friend Martin here, he had that the last time. Very delicious." With that he nodded toward Martin, smiled at them both, and walked briskly away toward the kitchen.

"I guess you come here often."

"Not as much as I'd like," Martin responded. "But it doesn't take many visits to make friends with Sal."

"That's the Sal your pizza choice is named after?"

"One and the same," Martin said with a grin. Then Martin's tone turned serious. He looked Jeff in the eye. "You have the same look on your face right now you had when I first saw you this morning, and it's not a happy look. What's going on with you?"

Earlier that day Jeff had thought he just wanted to be alone. Now he felt an overwhelming need for friendship and support. His work and family situations had been weighing more heavily on him than he had realized. He needed to release the burden he was carrying.

Suddenly Jeff found himself telling Martin about the year he would rather forget. At first he couldn't believe he was rehashing this whole saga, but Martin was so attentive, such a good listener, that Jeff kept talking.

He told him about the high expectations after the promotion and the disappointing relationship with his new boss. He talked about the frustrations of a colicky baby who rarely stopped crying, and he surprised himself when he even revealed the toll this was all taking on his relationship with his wife.

Martin listened quietly. Occasionally he asked a question, but for the most part he just listened.

Jeff felt good sharing his experience, but when he got to where he was today, he felt the weight of his situation and his anger toward Yvette bubbling back up.

"So today I have to hand in my performance evaluation. She has made it very clear to me that she thinks I'm screwing everything up. I know no matter what I say on my self-evaluation, she's going to want to go exploring and I'm going to want to scream. I feel totally lost."

Martin nodded his head. "It sounds like you're pretty angry with your boss."

"Of course I am." As he said these words, Jeff felt his voice rising and suddenly realized his hands were balled up into fists at his sides.

"Well, with a story like that, I don't blame you."

Jeff could feel the adrenaline surge as he thought about all the times Yvette had criticized him over the past six months. He was filled with indignation and was about to agree again with Martin. Yet there was something about the way Martin had said "story" that made Jeff pause and ask what he meant.

"Do you want to be angry?" Martin asked. "I mean, if you had a choice, would you choose to feel the way you feel now?"

"Of course not, but I can't just not be upset when that's what I feel."

"You're right about that," said Martin. "Some people say you can choose your feelings. I'm not sure I can do that, but I can control what gives me the feelings."

Jeff was curious about what Martin was getting at and again asked what he meant.

"What if I told you that your anger and stress and all the frustrations you just described aren't really a response to Yvette's actions?"

"I'd tell you you're crazy."

Martin chuckled. "You wouldn't be the first, but it's true. Your anger isn't a response to Yvette's actions. It's a response to your story."

Now Jeff was halfway between defensiveness at what he thought might be an accusation and curiosity to learn how he could let go of his frustration and negativity. Maybe it was just that he had nothing to lose, but Jeff let his guard down and once again asked Martin to explain.

"It's the stories you tell yourself that determine how you feel and act," Martin said. "Your stories are how you interpret the world around you. In fact, you are already a skilled storyteller. Unfortunately, you're telling the wrong stories."

Jeff was surprised by this. He was an avid reader of fiction and biographies and had always loved stories, but he had never been a very good writer.

"Now I know you're crazy. I can't tell a story to save my life."

"Well, *save* your life is a bit dramatic, but the stories you tell can definitely *change* your life. Three types of stories we all tell make us into heroes or victims. These stories are about other people, our situations, and ourselves. If you tell your stories the wrong way, they can make you miserable, angry, and unproductive. But if you master your stories — if you tell hero stories — they can make you feel happy and relaxed and even make you more effective and successful. Right now you are telling the wrong kinds of stories about Yvette and other challenges in your life."

> You tell three types of stories that make you
> a hero or a victim, stories about:
>
> Other people
> Your situation
> Yourself

A confused look crossed Jeff's face. Stories, heroes, and victims didn't sound real to him. It all sounded like something from a coming attraction for a movie. Jeff would soon discover just how real his stories were.

Other People's Challenges

The walls of the restaurant were covered with paintings of scenes from Italy. There was the Leaning Tower of Pisa, a gondolier in Venice, and a hilltop village. The old-world images combined with the conversation to give Jeff a surreal feeling. He imagined heroes and victims in centuries past, before the days of modern technology, office buildings, and performance reviews. He struggled to reconcile his image of heroes and victims with his own ordinary life.

Jeff turned to Martin and said, "I need a little help here. Stories, heroes, victims — what does all of that mean?"

"Let's take one thing at a time," Martin responded. "A story is anything you tell yourself to explain what you see. Let me give you an example of a story about people. Do customers ever make big requests of you, requests you might even call unreasonable?"

Jeff barked out a laugh, thinking about all of his clients who seemed to think he should be at their beck and call. It seemed not a day went by when someone didn't call with some kind of unrealistic demand.

"Sure," Jeff said. "I wish I had a few clients who didn't make unreasonable requests. They seem to think we sit around all day just waiting for them to call and we have no commitments other than to do whatever they want us to do whenever they want us to do it."

"So it sounds like you know what I'm describing. Well, let me tell you about a situation I ran into when I was working as a host in a restaurant during college. A couple walked in without a reservation. The husband said he had made a reservation, but we didn't have any record of that. Next he declared that he needed a table by the windows overlooking the park. Imagine an upscale restaurant with a crowd as big as you see here, and this guy wanted the table you and I are sitting at. We're talking about prime real estate."

Jeff looked around the restaurant. It was full and there was still a line out the door. He imagined what it would be like to be responsible for assigning the tables when everyone wanted to be seated right away. He didn't envy Martin's situation.

"We were packed," Martin continued, "and running a forty-five-minute wait for customers who did have reservations. So you can see it was going to be tough for me to accommodate this couple."

As Jeff imagined this scene, he looked over at the chefs working in the kitchen, enjoying the idea that he was sitting in the primo spot today.

"Yeah, that seems fair," Jeff said as he turned back to Martin. "If I had a reservation and was waiting for a table, I'd be pretty annoyed to see you walk that guy over to one of the prize tables when I still hadn't been seated."

"You're not alone there. I started to tell him I would do my best but it was going to take some time to seat him, well over an hour if he wanted a park view. Well, that set him off. He was furious we had lost his reservation. He accused me of not honoring our commitments. And I can assure you, he didn't say these things as nicely or calmly as I'm describing them to you."

Jeff laughed. "I'm sure he didn't. I'm embarrassed to admit it, but I'd be lying if I said I had never raised my voice with a restaurant host."

Martin smiled. "Don't worry. I won't hold it against you, but let me ask you a couple of questions. First, was this guy in the restaurant a jerk?"

"Obviously I don't know him, but I would say he was sure acting like a jerk. If he yells at you and accuses you of things that are unfair, I would say that makes him a jerk."

"OK. Now I have a question that may be unfair since I've set you up. Are you a jerk?"

Jeff raised his eyebrows quizzically. "What?"

"I'm going to assume by your surprise that you don't think you are a jerk. Yet you admitted you've also yelled at the host of a restaurant."

Now Jeff felt trapped. "Well, I've yelled, but I never—" Jeff stopped midstream. He realized he had no defense. He had been a jerk when he yelled at the restaurant host, and all of a sudden Jeff found he was laughing at himself. "I'm surprised to admit it, but you got me. I am officially a jerk."

"I don't think so," said Martin.

Jeff assumed he was just being nice now. So he said, "No, you're right. I've let a couple of people have it in restaurants. It was wrong of me. I was acting like a jerk."

"OK," said Martin. "That's a little different. You may have acted like a jerk in that situation, but you yourself aren't a jerk. This is an important difference because it has to do with your story."

As Martin finished speaking, two extremely delicious looking pizzas materialized in front of them. Looking up, Jeff saw Sal smiling down at them with a very satisfied look on his face.

"Here you go, my friends. You are about to be very happy. Enjoy."

Martin thanked him, and as Sal disappeared, Martin and Jeff took a moment to once again enjoy the aromas of the restaurant. The food in front of them looked like artwork. Each pizza was the size of a dinner plate and cut into quarters. Jeff reached down to take a slice from his pizza, and as he lifted it up he glanced across the table at Martin, who had a wide grin on his face.

"What?" asked Jeff.

"I think this moment is the happiest I've seen you today."

Jeff could have been embarrassed by this, but instead he

laughed and said, "You may be right, but I think I'm about to be even happier."

Jeff then dug into his pizza. Sal was right. It was sublime, and Jeff did indeed feel happier as he ate. Martin was true to his word. This pizza was the best he could ever remember tasting. Each flavor, each ingredient was perfectly blended with the others. The texture and consistency were perfect. The crust was nice and crispy, and the porcini mushrooms were deliciously seasoned.

Jeff was thoroughly enjoying his pizza, but he was also curious about something Martin had said. So he brought them back to their conversation.

"So explain to me why it's so important that I wasn't a jerk."

"OK. Let's go back to my example. What would happen to me when I was the host if I thought this guy demanding a window table was a jerk?"

"What do you mean, what would happen to you?"

"Well, first, how would I feel?"

Jeff thought for a moment about his experiences with his clients. He knew he had a pretty consistent reaction when they got demanding or angry with him.

"I know when my clients are jerks I get annoyed, frustrated, and even angry. If they yell at me or question my judgment, abilities, or motives I get really angry."

"That's right," said Martin. "So if I had gotten angry, what would that have done to my ability to do my job?"

"Well, I've seen enough hosts in crowded restaurants to know that you have to be calm and also give off a positive vibe. You're the first point of contact for the customer, and you need to start them off with a positive experience. So I guess the answer is that if you were angry, you would be a lot less effective at your job."

"What might I do in that case?"

Now Jeff remembered some of the scenes he had witnessed in restaurants over the years. It was a little embarrassing for him as he admitted to himself how many of these scenes he had contributed to.

Keeping the admission of guilt to himself, Jeff said, "You might yell back at the guy. You might have a sour look on your face when the next couple walks in the door. You could snap at the waiters if they did something you thought was wrong. It could trickle down to all kinds of behaviors."

"That's right. So if I tell myself this guy is a jerk, I make myself less happy and less effective at my work. If I tell myself lots of people are jerks, then over time I'll stop caring about my customers altogether. I will be a lot less successful."

Jeff had spent time working in sales and customer service at his company, and he had seen many people fall into this mindset. They didn't want to answer the phones, assuming every new caller would be difficult or stupid or not worth their time. Even minor customer complaints would set them off. Still, he knew that not every customer was a pleasure to deal with.

"I've seen this happen at my company," Jeff said. "So I think I get what you are saying, but this guy was a jerk. He didn't have a reservation. There was a forty-five-minute wait and he wanted to be seated immediately in one of the premier seats in the restaurant. That's a jerk."

"No," said Martin. "That's a story. You are telling yourself a story about this person that's making you angry even now."

Jeff sat back in his chair for a moment and realized Martin was right. There he was, sitting in this restaurant. All he was doing was talking about an incident that happened a long time ago, and it hadn't even happened to him. Yet he was getting angry.

The facts were simple. A couple had entered the restaurant. The man had claimed he had a reservation. Martin didn't see any record of the reservation, and the man had become upset.

Then Jeff had piled his story on top of the facts. This guy was inconsiderate. He was unreasonable. He was probably a liar. He was a jerk. As he thought about it, Jeff was surprised at how quickly and easily he was able to construct a story that was this upsetting.

"You're right. I am feeling angry. I would laugh at myself if I wasn't feeling so aggravated."

"That's a perfect example of what a victim story can do," Martin replied. "When we are victims, we tell ourselves stories that bring us down, make us angry, and steal our ability to face our challenges. It is amazing how quickly your stories can make you into a victim and steal your happiness. Even now your stories are preventing you from laughing."

Jeff didn't like the idea of something stealing his happiness, especially if that something came from inside of him. He asked Martin to explain the new story he could tell.

"Sure," Martin said. "To change your story, you switch from a victim to a hero. Heroic stories lift you up, energize you, and give you the ability to take positive actions. Heroes are people who, even in the most challenging situations, stay positive and find ways to work to overcome their challenges. Heroes see other people through a different lens. So if you are angry with someone or might get angry with them, put yourself in a heroic state of mind. Ask yourself, what would the hero see?"

"What would the hero see?" repeated Jeff. "What does that mean?"

"Think about what we've discussed and you tell me," replied Martin.

Jeff thought about heroes. There were the obvious heroes — Superman, Wonder Woman. Then he thought about heroes in the real world — nurses, firefighters, and teachers. There seemed to be a clear theme.

"When I think of heroes, they seem to be focused not on themselves but on the people around them. They see what other people are going through and where they need help."

"You've got it," said Martin. "They see other people's challenges, needs, and pain."

Jeff thought about how he responded to Yvette. She said and did a lot of things that made him angry. She criticized him. She didn't understand him. She was a general pain.

So what was he seeing? In that moment it became clear to him in a hurry.

"Right now I see really clearly all the ways Yvette is hurting me."

"That's good," said Martin. "You see your own pain and challenges. That's what the victim sees. If you were seeing what the hero sees, you would see her pain and challenges. That would make all the difference."

People Stories

Victims focus on their own pain and tell stories that blame others.
Ask, **what would the hero see?**
to connect you with other people's challenges.

Jeff gave this some thought. What Yvette might be feeling, other than anger toward Jeff, had never even crossed his mind. He had never considered the stress she might be under. He had never thought of her as someone who might be facing tough challenges of her own. Still, he wasn't convinced.

"That seems awfully simple," Jeff said.

"Does it? Let's see about that. It's certainly easy to assume the worst. It's easy to see the guy in the restaurant as just an angry and belligerent jerk. But what if you forced yourself to consider other options? Tell me what story you would tell about him if you were seeing like a hero."

Jeff thought Martin's question was kind of silly. The guy obviously needed a table, and he was just being demanding. Jeff didn't see any other ways to view the guy. Then he smiled as he thought of one possibility.

"Does hunger count as a pain?"

Martin laughed. "Count? I consider it one of my major drivers in life, but I know you can come up with more than that. What else could you see if you were the hero? What other challenges might this guy have been experiencing?"

When Martin said this, Jeff imagined himself going out with Marie. Suddenly the picture became much clearer for him. "Maybe it's a special occasion for him and his wife."

"Go on," Martin said.

"It could be their anniversary. Maybe they don't go out very often for nice meals."

Martin gave an encouraging nod and waited for Jeff to continue.

Jeff thought for another moment. Now he was getting into it. "They don't go out much because they have a new baby. In fact, they haven't gone out to dinner together, just the two of them, for over a year. Their baby cries all the time. So they are always stressed out."

Jeff was picking up steam. "He knows his wife is afraid of staying too long at the restaurant because they have never left the baby for that long. All he wanted was one nice night out with his wife, one special experience before going home to a screaming baby and what could be another year of living with a stressed-out family and no personal time—another whole year before they get to go out together again for just one nice night out. And now it's all getting ruined, and he's watching it crumble before his eyes."

When Jeff finished, he saw Martin was smiling. He realized he had been speaking with some intensity. "I guess I got a little carried away," he said sheepishly, knowing how close to home his story was.

"Not at all," said Martin. "You're right on track. Now tell me. How do you feel about the guy you just described?"

"I feel bad for him."

"Tell me more."

"Well, I still don't think it's right for him to yell at you, but I'm not angry. I want to help him — help him calm down, take away some of his pain."

"So if that's how you feel about him, how would you act toward him?"

Jeff imagined how he would want someone to take care of him. He thought about the stress he and Marie would have felt had they been the couple in that restaurant.

He said, "I might look for different solutions. Maybe he could get seated more quickly if I could get him to relax on needing a table by the window. Maybe I would get him a drink on the house. I don't know what else a host can do, but I'd want to try something."

"Good," said Martin. "Now, if that's how you feel toward him and those are some of the things you try to do for him, how do you feel about yourself?"

Jeff was a little surprised. He had been so focused on the other guy in his story he had totally forgotten about himself. "I guess I feel pretty good. I mean here I am helping out this guy who is feeling awful and stressed out. That feels pretty good."

"You've got it."

At that moment there was a crash of breaking glass a few tables away. Someone had knocked a water glass off of their table. A waiter rushed over with a towel, got to work cleaning the mess, and assured the apologetic customer it was OK. Jeff wished every mess could be so easily cleaned up.

"All right," Jeff said, "then I have a couple of questions."

"Fire away," Martin said.

"So does this just mean the squeaky wheel gets the oil?" Jeff asked. "Am I just training myself to give people who are acting out exactly what they want?"

"Not necessarily. Just because you see like a hero doesn't mean you can or will ease everyone's pain. But it does allow you to feel calm when dealing with people who might otherwise make you angry. In my situation I didn't get angry, and I was happy when I moved on from him to my next customer."

Again Jeff thought about the sales and customer service representatives at his company. There were people in those departments who leaped to pick up the phone when it rang and were calm when calls ended. Jeff had always thought it was just personality differences that made some people respond more positively. Now he wondered if it was their stories that made that difference.

Martin continued, "My stories told me every unhappy customer had the weight of the world on his or her shoulders. With so much pressure and stress, they were bound to blow up at some point. That didn't mean they all got what they wanted from me. It did mean I could feel for them and not make assumptions that they were all jerks."

Jeff thought for a moment, absorbing this idea. The heroic story didn't force him to give people what they wanted. Rather, it helped him to stay calm. That would allow him to respond effectively, make better decisions, and be more successful in his job. He'd even be happier.

Martin broke into his thoughts. "Did you have another question?"

"Yeah. This story is all well and good, but in the end it is just a story. It's probably not true. Why should I pay attention to this story?"

"That's a good question. Let me ask a question in return. Is your original story, the one in which you thought the guy in the restaurant was a jerk, any more likely to be true than this one is?"

Jeff squirmed in his chair. He thought about his own story that this guy was inconsiderate, even a liar. He had to admit to himself that he had no idea what the real truth was. This suddenly brought home to him how much he was guiding himself based on stories that were quite likely incorrect. He managed a shake of his head. Martin took this as a signal to continue.

"OK. So we don't know what story is correct. Even if you know someone is consistently critical, self-absorbed, or hostile, you don't know what is leading them to those actions. But you do have a choice. You can select a story that makes you angry, ineffective, and unhappy or a story that makes you happy, caring, and successful. If neither story is any more likely than the other to be correct, why wouldn't you choose the one that makes you into a hero instead of a victim? The hero story makes you happy and effective. The victim story just makes you angry."

Jeff realized Martin was right. Jeff was clinging to the story that made him angry even though it was probably not true. What he didn't realize was that the lessons were only going to get harder.

Red-Carpet Treatment

The lunchtime rush was in full swing, and the restaurant was buzzing. The patrons sitting at their tables were content, enjoying the atmosphere. Those waiting for tables craned their necks, impatiently watching for diners to pay their checks and signal their imminent departure.

Surveying the scene, Martin said, "You've done well finding the heroic stories I could have told as the host of the restaurant. Now it's time to look at this from a different angle. What story was the other guy telling?"

"You want to know the story that the guy who wanted the window table was telling?" Jeff asked. Martin nodded his head.

"Well, he wasn't happy with you. He probably thought you lost his reservation. You weren't very competent. You weren't trying hard to help him. He probably thought you were a jerk."

"That seemed easy for you to come up with," Martin said with a smile.

Jeff also smiled this time, as he thought about the times he had gotten angry with restaurant hosts. "Too easy," he replied sheepishly.

"So change his story. What story would he tell if he used our question?"

Jeff reconsidered the question that changes his story: What would the hero see? After imagining this perspective for a few moments, he described the new story for Martin.

"You had been yelled at a dozen times already that night by people who didn't want to wait. There were more than a few regulars and celebrities who expected special treatment. No one at a window table was even close to finishing their meal. People came to the restaurant all the time claiming to have made reservations when in fact they never made them. To top it all off, you had gotten in a huge fight with your girlfriend right before coming to work that day."

Jeff leaned back and smiled at what he considered to be a well-crafted story.

Martin nodded his head. "That's not bad at all. You're getting the hang of this."

"I can see how the guy would have acted totally differently if that had been his story. He might have simply said nothing, or he might have explained his situation and why it was so important to him to have a window table or to be seated quickly."

"Right," Martin said. "He would have felt different. He would have acted differently, and he would have gotten better results."

"What do you mean by better results?"

"Well, I did make sure this guy had a good night, but his night would have been a whole lot better if he had appealed to me without blowing his top. See, I want to take care of people when I see they are struggling, but I want to take care of them even more if they show me their struggles without taking their frustration out on me.

"So I told this guy I could seat him as though he had a reservation, which still put him at a forty-five-minute wait. I could only give him a window table if he was willing to wait an hour and a half. Since I knew that was unacceptable to him, I offered something to make the night special. I told him I would get him a copy of the menu, autographed by the chef. This restaurant had a pretty well known chef, and the guy liked that idea a lot.

"Now, if he hadn't yelled at me but had simply told me his story, I might have done more for him. He got an autographed copy of the menu, but he could have gotten a visit to his table from the chef. The autograph would have been personalized. He might have gotten a complimentary dessert or a dish off the menu prepared specially for him."

"Wow," said Jeff. "I didn't realize how many perks a happy host can bestow on his patrons. Or should I say a heroic host?"

"You could say that. I'm sure it's the same with you. You probably have lots of things you can do for your clients. Sometimes you give them the red-carpet treatment, and sometimes you don't."

Jeff thought about some of his clients and how he treated them. He definitely had a broad range of ways he could take care of them. Recently he received a call from a new manager named Travis. Jeff almost immediately labeled the guy as pushy and demanding. It was all downhill from there.

Travis wanted an exception to allow someone from his office to attend a special company event. Jeff put Travis's request at the bottom of his to-do list. It must have taken Jeff two weeks to get back to him with an answer, and that was just to tell him there was nothing Jeff could do. He certainly didn't put up any fight anywhere along the way to help Travis get what he wanted.

Thinking back on his actions made Jeff feel a little guilty. Travis was new and probably still trying to figure out the way things worked. Jeff could have helped him in his struggles, but instead he made Travis's situation worse. Beyond that, Jeff's actions didn't just hurt Travis. The person who really lost out was the person in Travis's office, who might have been highly deserving, but Jeff had never thought of that.

"I realize now I've been thinking of a lot of my clients as jerks lately. I've been telling myself all the wrong stories, and I haven't been treating them as well as I could or maybe should."

Martin said, "That's an important thing to recognize. I can see you're already getting the hang of seeing what the hero would see. So now it's time for the real test. It's time for you to tell a story about what the hero would see in Yvette."

Yvette's Pain

Jeff thought about Yvette and tried to come up with heroic stories. He hadn't considered her needs or challenges for a very long time. As he was thinking, Sal returned to take their plates away and offer dessert and coffee. Jeff noticed both his and Martin's plates were practically licked clean, and at Martin's suggestion, he agreed to some biscotti but passed on the coffee.

Jeff was glad he had made an effort to get extra work done that morning to clear space for this time with Martin. He recognized this conversation was doing him a lot of good. He wasn't convinced Martin had solved his problems, but he was certainly feeling like there might be a light at the end of this tunnel.

Jeff looked at Martin and nodded his head, acknowledging he was as ready as he was going to get to deal with Yvette.

Martin leaned forward in his chair. "Before you try to work out a new story, tell me what story you are telling about Yvette now."

Jeff thought about the guy who wanted the window table in Martin's restaurant and some of the clients who had gotten under his skin lately. He thought about how he had labeled them jerks for their behavior. Then he thought about how he had reacted to Yvette, and the answer was clear.

"I'm telling a victim story. I'm convincing myself that she is a jerk."

"How so?" Martin asked.

"She's a jerk because she is so critical of me. She doesn't care about the fact that I am new in this job and could use some guidance from her. She doesn't recognize how hard I'm working to try to keep everything running at a high level. She's a jerk because she invited me here and then she practically abandoned me to my work. She wanted me to be on her team and then she treated me like a leper. She doesn't care about me at all."

Martin shook his head as he said, "That's a story that's bound to make you angry."

"But it's not just a story," Jeff replied. As he said it he could hear the whine in his voice and was immediately embarrassed by how weak his comment sounded in his own ears.

Now Martin looked Jeff straight in the eye. Jeff couldn't hold his gaze. He had to look away. Jeff was a fidgeter by nature, and this behavior tended to escalate when he was uncomfortable or struggling with something. He suddenly found himself rearranging the salt and pepper shakers on the table in front of him.

After a minute he turned back to Martin and said, "All right. It is a story, but it feels true to me."

"That's fine. Actually, it's perfect," replied Martin. "It's important to realize that any time you have a story with no alternatives, it will feel true to you. Strong emotions — frustration, aggravation, defensiveness — can be clues that you need to look for an alternate story. You need to see what the hero would see."

"But isn't it possible I really am a victim in this situation?

Isn't it possible she has treated me poorly? That I got a raw deal?"

Martin looked at Jeff with eyes that seemed to read his thoughts. Jeff squirmed under the scrutiny and eventually broke the gaze and went back to shuffling the salt and pepper shakers.

Finally Martin spoke. "It's possible you've been mistreated, but in the end only you can make yourself into a victim. You can choose the stories of the victim or you can choose the stories of the hero. When you are deep in the victim stories, it can be difficult, even excruciating, to find the hero stories. But the choice remains yours. So now tell me: what would the hero see in Yvette?"

"I wish I knew," Jeff replied, "because I'd love to see her through new eyes."

"Don't give up on me now," challenged Martin. "What pain could cause her to do the things that have made you so angry? Let's start with your feeling that she has abandoned you. Did you always feel that way?"

Jeff shook his head.

"So tell me some stories about a pain in her life that could have caused these new behaviors?"

Jeff found himself fighting against the new stories. "I think I can come up with something, but now I realize part of me doesn't want to. It's like I don't want to discover a story that will make me give up my anger."

"That happens all the time," Martin replied. "We want to hold onto the stories that are comfortable for us and reinforce what we've already decided. Now that you recognize that tendency, it should be easier for you to let go."

Before Jeff could respond, Sal appeared with a plate of assorted biscotti and a cup of cappuccino with a beautiful frothed top. As he watched Martin spoon some sugar into the cappuccino, he thought, as he had many times in the past, it would be nice to share this experience. So many people seemed passionate about coffee, but he just couldn't bring himself to like it.

"Jeff!"

As he heard Martin calling his name, he realized he had been zoning out, watching the coffee and avoiding the challenge at hand. He snapped his head up to see Martin smiling reassuringly at him.

"What we are discussing is a big step," Martin said. "Do you want to tackle this now or should we call it a day on the hero talk?"

Jeff thought about it. It would be wonderful to just forget this conversation and stick with his current views. The idea of continuing his anger toward Yvette — blaming her for his frustrations — felt so safe to him. But he also knew he was too far along to do that. If he took that approach now, he would know it was a lie, and he would hate himself even more than he hated Yvette.

"No," replied Jeff. "I can't call it a day yet. The truth is I could come up with a million stories."

"Good. Tell me what comes to mind first."

Still resisting, Jeff added the sugar bowl and a Parmesan shaker to his arrangement of salt and pepper and was reaching for the hot pepper flakes, which would have provided a nice addition to the condiment city he was creating. Instead, he pulled his hand back, shook his head, and focused.

"Well, Yvette is always in meetings with very senior people in the organization. She could be getting more assignments that are pulling on her time. She could know about things such as mergers or acquisitions coming down the pike that could influence her department. Maybe something is coming that could lead to layoffs, and she is off fighting for me and my team to keep our jobs."

Jeff suddenly felt very guilty. "Wow! What if all the time I've been thinking she was a jerk she was actually trying to save me?"

Martin gave him a thoughtful look. "It is amazing how our

stories can change the way we view people. Tell me some more stories for the other issues you described."

"OK," Jeff said. Now the stories were coming more easily. "Maybe she has been critical of me lately because she thinks I can handle it. Or maybe she just doesn't have time for some of the more supportive conversations because of the demands of her new cross-functional team."

"Those are good. Think about yourself for a second. Have you been as effective while sleep deprived as you were before your daughter was born?"

"Are you kidding me?" Jeff laughed. "Some days I think a chimpanzee would be more effective than me."

Martin laughed at this but returned to a serious expression. "I don't want to suggest that you should get a pass for any mistakes or poor performance, but isn't it reasonable that people should take your situation into consideration when evaluating your actions?"

"I suppose so."

"Well, if other people should consider your life circumstances, shouldn't we do the same for Yvette? What could be happening in her life that could make her less effective as your manager?"

Jeff had never thought about that. Again he discovered he was rearranging the condiments. When he looked up, Martin's gaze made it clear he was expecting an answer.

"OK," said Jeff. "There could be all kinds of stories. She could be having difficulty with her marriage or dealing with her kids leaving for college or who knows — she could even be going through some kind of medical issues."

"That's good," said Martin. "Would those stories help you feel more caring toward her?"

"Sure," Jeff said sheepishly.

"OK. Now here's the toughest part to consider. What stories would you tell if you were the one causing Yvette pain?"

Jeff looked over at the kitchen. He didn't want to answer Martin's question, but he had come this far.

"I guess the story would be…"

Jeff didn't know how to finish this sentence. He didn't know how it happened, but when Jeff looked down he discovered he was holding salt in one hand and Parmesan in the other. He quickly put down the shakers and searched for the source of his discomfort.

"With all of these other stories," Jeff finally said, "I could excuse Yvette's behavior as something having to do with her. I didn't realize you were going to come back around to me."

"It is always hardest to see a new story about ourselves, and like the others, it may or may not be true. But you were criticized by someone you trust and respect, or at least you used to. When that happens, one story you should consider is how you might be the source of that person's pain."

Jeff didn't know how to hide from this. So instead he gave it his best shot. "If I am the source of her pain, it might be because my performance has been subpar. Maybe I haven't shown as much skill or been as independent or as quick a learner as I should have been in this role. Or maybe Yvette is OK with my performance, but she just needed to critique me, and I'm blowing things out of proportion."

Martin picked up an almond biscotti and took a bite, his eyes gazing toward the front of the restaurant. Jeff again thought of the way Martin reminded him of the look the Guru had described to him. He looked completely at peace.

Martin turned back to Jeff. "We've covered a lot of ground. Now I think it's time for both of us to go back to work."

This had been a wonderful lunch and Jeff didn't want it to end. Suddenly something occurred to him.

"Wait a second. Earlier you said there were three stories that could change my life. We've only talked about one."

"That's right," Martin said with raised eyebrows. "You have

a good memory. We've talked about the story you can tell about other people. And the question that goes along with that story is, what would the hero see? You should also know that each story builds strength within you that leads to greater happiness and success. The story about other people builds the strength of empathy. The victim feels resentment toward others. The hero feels empathy."

> *Heroic stories about other people build empathy.*

"If you are still interested in the other two stories, I'll be back in your building tomorrow. My meetings should end at ten o'clock. How about meeting in the lobby again at ten fifteen?"

"I'll be there," Jeff said. Martin insisted on paying for lunch. Once they were outside he wished Jeff luck with Yvette and hopped into a cab.

Jeff stood there for another minute and thought through his conversation and what he had learned. He thought about the stories he had been telling and how he frequently played the victim, but rarely, if ever, did he see others' pain.

Then he thought again about Yvette. He was shocked to discover he actually wanted to talk to her, and not just talk to her but listen to her, work harder for her, find more ways to help her.

What was even more shocking was Jeff realized he actually felt good. He felt good about Yvette and he felt good about himself. He was eager to see her and to see the rest of his team, but what he was most eager for was to see Martin again. As excited as Jeff was, even he would be surprised at what he would have to tell Martin the following day.

New Discoveries

Jeff walked back into his office ready to tackle his performance appraisal. He felt none of the oppression he had felt earlier that morning. He dove right in and was surprised to discover that the ratings and comments were coming more easily to him.

He stopped at one point to think about what was different and realized it was all about his stories. Earlier that morning Jeff had paralyzed himself by being a victim. What did Yvette think of him? How would she evaluate him? He had been mired in trying to interpret stories he didn't even know were true.

This time he started with a hero's perspective, a viewpoint that told him Yvette might be facing challenges of her own. From that perspective, he could believe Yvette valued him and valued honesty. All she would really want to hear was what he believed to be true. With that story in mind, Jeff simply wrote from his heart.

He was about halfway through when Greg, one of the people on his team, popped his head into Jeff's office.

"Got a minute, Skippy?" Greg liked to have a little fun with the fact that he was nearly twice Jeff's age. He usually did this by calling Jeff various creative nicknames. Currently Skippy was in vogue.

Looking up from his appraisal form, Jeff said, "Sure, Greg. What's up?"

When Greg sat down, Jeff knew what was coming. Jeff was by no means expert at reading people, but Greg would have to be the world's worst poker player. Whenever he was nervous, his skin turned not quite crimson but noticeably red. Just in case his audience was blind enough not to notice this, his nervousness also led him to clear his throat repeatedly before speaking.

Jeff waited patiently through the symphony of "ah-hums."

Finally Greg said, "I'll just cut to the chase. I need another few days on the South East proposal."

Jeff tried not to roll his eyes. That proposal was already late, the second missed deadline having been the previous Friday. Jeff felt a surge of anger, thinking about how Greg dragged him down. He never tried hard enough and didn't seem to care how his delays made Jeff look.

"Greg," Jeff said. "This just isn't . . ."

If anything, Greg's color was getting redder in anticipation of Jeff's rebuke, but Jeff stopped and sat there, his mouth open, his sentence unfinished.

Suddenly his lunch conversation flashed before his eyes, and he realized how many stories he had just told about Greg. Martin's voice played in his head.

"What would the hero see?" he heard Martin ask.

After a brief struggle to shift his frame of mind, Jeff found a new story flowing through his head. The hero would see Greg's pain, would recognize Greg was afraid of failure. He delayed because he was concerned he might have missed something or needed things to be perfect. His perfectionism was driven by a deep concern for his clients, his team, and even for Jeff, his boss.

With the new story Jeff felt different. He wanted to help Greg, who after all was just a guy who was trying his best and was in over his head. In that moment Jeff realized how angry, impatient, and pushy he had been with Greg in the past. He hadn't given Greg the support that would help him improve his performance.

"Uh, Earth to Skippy? Come in, Skippy." Across the desk, Greg looked almost worried.

Then in a near out-of-body experience, Jeff watched himself say something that would have been unthinkable only hours before.

"Tell me, Greg. What can I do to help you make this proposal all you want it to be?"

Greg had clearly been bracing for the usual shoving match and demands for quick turnaround. It took him a few seconds to readjust and figure out how to respond, but he wasn't the only one. Jeff had shocked himself with his question. What happened next was an upbeat, energized, productive exchange about what Greg needed to do and how Jeff could support Greg's needs.

When Greg eventually left his office, Jeff had an epiphany. He had assumed for a long time that Greg didn't care about his work, but that was the victim's perspective. He suddenly realized that very few people go to work each day determined to do a bad job. People generally want to do their best. They want to succeed.

Then he remembered a conversation from the prior week, when he ran into a couple of other people from his team. They were complaining about a group in another department. As Jeff replayed the conversation in his mind, he realized two things.

First, all of their complaints were victim stories like the ones Jeff had told himself about Greg. They were criticisms about how the other group didn't care as much as Jeff's group, how they didn't try as hard, or how their work just wasn't as good. These stories were driven by and subsequently created anger, bitterness, and rivalry between the groups.

The second realization for Jeff was that most of their stories were ones Jeff had also told, and now he regretted doing so.

He thought about his time in the rotation program and about how people in one department didn't trust the people in other departments. The people in marketing said the sales people didn't try hard enough to work with the messages they created. In sales they said marketing didn't understand what their job was like.

It was the same with sales and human resources or human resources and finance. Every department told stories about every other department, but Jeff had worked in almost all departments. They were filled with hard-working people who really wanted to do their best for the company. He was struck again by the idea that people are frequently misunderstood, but for the most part, they want to do their best.

Just as earlier he had been surprised to find the Parmesan shaker in his hand, now Jeff picked up his phone and started dialing before he even realized what he was doing. When someone picked up on the other end, the words came naturally to Jeff.

"Wendy," he said, "it's Jeff. Are you free for lunch next Wednesday? It's been way too long since we last got together. I'd like to share some ideas with you and talk about how our teams might be able to work better together."

Wendy agreed, and as Jeff hung up, he thought about how his organization would change if everyone saw through heroes' eyes. He imagined how much more effective the company would be. Suddenly he imagined people in different departments and work groups and regions telling stories about the effort and concerns and struggles of other groups.

People would be more supportive of one another. There would be more collaboration and open communication. People would give one another the benefit of the doubt and reduce or even eliminate petty office politics.

As his mind drifted through these images of what a heroic company would be like, his computer chirped with a task reminder that his performance appraisal was due that day. So he dove back in and before long put the finishing touches on it. With less trepidation than he expected, he walked the papers down to Yvette's office.

She was having coffee, of course, and was therefore in good spirits.

After Jeff handed her his forms, she thanked him and told him she was looking forward to seeing what he wrote. One part of Jeff wanted to tell her about his morning, about the revelations he had experienced, but another part wanted to wait, to see how she responded to his appraisal once she had read it. In the end, neither part of Jeff made the decision. Yvette's phone rang, and she asked Jeff to excuse her so she could take the call.

As he left her office he realized he felt pretty good — about himself, about Yvette, and about his job. Unfortunately, he would soon discover there were limits to how his new stories about other people could improve his life.

Seeing Marie Anew

On his way home Jeff thought about his family. He started with Marie. He felt awful admitting it to himself, but he had told terrible stories about her. Being a husband and a father was tougher than people told him it would be. There were times when Marie drove him crazy.

On top of that, it had been a long nine months since Siena was born, with nearly nonstop crying ever since. At first it didn't matter how much she cried. He and Marie were just deliriously happy to have her in the world. They loved everything about her even when she was screaming her little head off.

But after a couple months, the crying began to get to Jeff. He started to feel less and less eager to take care of her when she started screaming. So he began pushing Marie to do more, not directly but in a lot of subtle or not-so-subtle ways. He'd find reasons he had to work late or would pretend to be asleep when Siena cried at night.

He realized he had been justifying all of these actions with victim stories. He was telling himself that Marie didn't appreciate how hard he worked. She didn't care about him nearly as much as she cared about Siena. She didn't pay attention to any of his needs. He was telling himself stories that made her out to be a jerk so he wouldn't feel so bad about how he was treating her.

Traffic was moving slowly, and Jeff began to wonder about how Marie viewed herself. He was quite certain she didn't think of herself as unappreciative or uncaring or unwilling to put in equal effort. In fact, he knew if he so much as whispered one of those accusations in her presence, he would be sleeping on the couch for a week.

"What are her stories about me?"

After the words came out of his mouth he looked around as if concerned there might be someone else in his car to overhear his question. Finding he was still alone, he thought about his question.

He thought about how he did care. He did appreciate Marie's work. More importantly, he did make an effort to help with Siena and to make their relationship thrive. He may have had moments when he wasn't the perfect husband or father, but overall he tried to do a good job in both of those roles.

"I'm not a villain," he said to himself, this time not bothering to check the car for phantom passengers.

In that moment he realized he was almost never the villain in the stories he told about himself. Thinking about Marie, he was pretty sure she didn't see herself as the villain either.

He had cast plenty of people as villains during his life — girlfriends, his parents at times, former coworkers. In each of these relationships his stories created distance — a distance he now recognized between himself and Marie.

"If I make myself into a victim with Marie, I make her a villain. Our stories are almost certainly opposed to one another. If I see what the hero sees, I will tell a more positive story about her. Neither of us will be a villain or a victim, and our stories will bring us closer rather than drive us apart."

Jeff smiled at this realization and considered how many arguments over the years he might have averted if he had thought this way, if he had seen what the hero sees. Lost in his thoughts, he almost passed the shopping plaza.

In the plaza was Groove, a music memorabilia and used CD store. Marie's interest in music was insatiable. Groove was on his drive home and very convenient. Every time he passed the store, it reminded him of how he frequently bought gifts for Marie when they were first dating. He called it the random gift. He never needed an occasion. He just loved to surprise Marie with little items that might make her happy.

For the last year, whenever he passed Groove, he convinced himself he was too late, exhausted, angry, or something. For twelve months he hadn't once bought anything for his wife, all the while telling himself he would get something the next week.

Today Jeff stopped and bought a CD featuring Yo-Yo Ma, Marie's favorite cellist. As he paid for the gift, Jeff thought about the year that had passed. It had been tough on him, but now, for the first time, he considered how it must have been for Marie.

Everything he had struggled with she had, too. Plus she had given birth, dealt with breast feeding and hormone shifts, and tried to get her body back in shape — and all of this with a husband who was suddenly working longer hours than ever before.

The farther into the new story he got, the more he wanted to take care of her and show her how much he loved her. He could barely wait to get home.

When he walked through the door of his house, he wondered why he hadn't done this more often. Marie was shocked when Jeff pulled out the CD.

"What is this for?" she asked with a blazing smile on her face.

"Not what. Who? It's for you, because I love you," Jeff responded.

After Marie put the CD into the computer and set it to play, Jeff led her to the couch. It was a rare moment in which Siena was occupied and they had relative peace. As the deep tones of the cello drifted through the air, Jeff told Marie how much he appreciated her and recognized the difficulties she had faced this year.

"I know this has been a tough time for you — as much as or more than it has for me. I just want you to know how much you mean to me and how wonderful I think you have been with Siena."

Marie put her head on Jeff's shoulder as a tear slipped down her cheek, and Jeff wrapped his arms around her.

The peacefulness of that moment was certainly different from the usual experience, Jeff thought. As though she could read his mind, Siena chose that moment to start crying, and Jeff reluctantly broke his embrace with Marie to attend to the baby.

Throughout the evening, Jeff found that he and Marie were more caring with one another than they had been for some time. For most of the night, Jeff was convinced the new stories he was telling could work miracles. Unfortunately, he soon found that even miracles have their limits.

Losing the Story

Siena went through her usual crying spell from six to nine and then went to bed. Going to bed for her consisted of Jeff carrying her back and forth across her room about a hundred times until she fell asleep. Then he placed her delicately in her crib and prayed she wouldn't wake up when he put her down. All during this time he was more patient than usual as he thought about how the hero would view Siena. He focused on what pain she might be experiencing.

This night she stayed asleep on the first try. So Jeff was able to spend a few minutes of quality time with Marie before they both collapsed into bed exhausted, wondering how long they would be allowed to sleep that night.

As it turned out, it wasn't long. At eleven thirty Siena was up and demanding attention. This time Jeff jumped up to take care of her, determined to be empathic no matter how much she cried.

He thought about his victim stories. The stories he had told for the last several months were that Siena was a difficult or an angry baby. At the worst of times he told stories that she was manipulative and mean.

This night he asked himself, what would the hero see? Maybe something was wrong physically. Maybe her little body was actually feeling pain. Or maybe she was frightened and needed her family, her pack. She was a defenseless little creature who was afraid of the dark and being alone.

And the new stories worked. He felt empathy big time. He was concerned, he was extra tender and caring—for the first hour.

By twelve thirty Jeff started to lose touch with his new, empathic story and just wanted the crying to stop. He found himself slipping back into his old stories. The exhaustion started to take over, and his frustration and anger surged.

Jeff did what he had to do. He cared for her until she fell asleep another hour later, but by then he was angry, bitter, and resentful toward Siena and Marie and the world.

When Siena started crying again at three o'clock, he gave a not so gentle nudge to Marie. Even with Marie going to Siena, her screaming kept him up. By the time his alarm rang to wake him for work, he was as exhausted as ever.

Jeff took his usual morning anger to work with him that day, and at ten o'clock he was sitting at his desk debating whether or not to see Martin again. He was frustrated with his night and had nearly convinced himself that the stories he had learned the day before were useless.

Then Greg walked past his office and gave Jeff a big wave and grin. Remembering his conversation yesterday with Greg brought back the positive outcomes that had resulted from his new stories. They hadn't cured everything, but they seemed to be worth a second look.

So, with some reluctance, Jeff headed down to the lobby. When he stepped out of the elevator, he saw Martin standing with a couple of other people. As he walked closer, he recognized that the people Martin was speaking with were senior executives in his company. He had shaken hands with each of them during his time in the rotation program, but he had never had the kind of comfortable conversation Martin was clearly having with them.

Jeff started to veer off so as not to interrupt their conversation, but Martin had seen him and was waving him over. With a deep gulp, Jeff walked over and tried his best to look confident.

When Jeff arrived, Martin said, "Brenda, Alex, this is Jeff, an old friend of mine and one of the graduates of your Fast Track program. Jeff, this is Brenda, your chief operating officer, and Alex, your chief financial officer."

Each of them shook his hand while Brenda said, "You have a very impressive friend, Jeff. It's no wonder you were a Fast Tracker. I imagine you'll be taking my job some day."

"Not so fast, Brenda," Alex said. "I'm not going to work here forever. Who says he won't take my job?"

They were both smiling warmly, and Jeff was doing his best not to show the sense of awe he felt in this company.

"I can only dare to dream," he responded.

Then Alex turned back to Martin: "Thank you again for the session this morning, Martin. This is going to completely reshape the way we work together as a team."

"Not to mention," Brenda chimed in, "how we lead each of our departments. I can assure you everyone is very eager to hear what comes next."

Martin shook hands with each of them. "It has been my pleasure. You all are doing wonderful work here. I can't wait to see more of the outcomes, but all in due time. I'll see you again soon."

They said their goodbyes, and Brenda and Alex again shook Jeff's hand and wished him well. Then they headed out the door, leaving Jeff in even more awe of his old friend.

He was still looking out the door where they had left when Martin said to him, "The flies are going to get in."

Jeff realized his mouth was agape and quickly snapped it shut. "How do you know them? Are you teaching them about seeing like a hero, too? The executive team is learning this stuff?"

"Whoa! Hold on there. Yes, I'm doing some work with them, but what I do with them is a surprise only they are allowed to reveal."

Jeff shook his head and stared out beyond the doors where Brenda and Alex had left the building. He could see pedestrians moving briskly, traffic flowing, and buildings competing with one another for height and style honors.

Looking at the scene, he remembered how he used to feel when he first moved to the city. He would marvel at the beauty of it, the energy, the diversity. He still loved those things, but he had taken them for granted lately. For a moment he allowed himself to soak up the view while he wondered what Martin might be doing with these executives.

He thought again of the company he had imagined, in which everyone told hero stories. He felt proud of the way he had already used these stories to shift his actions and relationships with Greg and Wendy.

He was lost in daydreams when Martin said, "It is exciting, isn't it?"

Jeff wasn't sure what Martin was describing, but he replied, "Yes, it is."

After another moment Jeff turned to Martin.

"I have some surprises to share," Jeff said.

"Go ahead."

"You helped me see how I was telling a victim story with Yvette yesterday, but you didn't tell me how many other stories there were."

After a long pause Martin said, "Go on."

"OK. I left here yesterday prepared to change my story about Yvette. I didn't realize I would be changing my stories in almost every encounter I had."

Jeff proceeded to share his experiences from the prior day. As he reviewed his day, he was pleased to share all of the triumphs he had experienced — with Greg, Wendy, Yvette, Marie, and Siena. Then he got to the end of the story and finished on a down note.

"For some reason the story didn't work," he concluded.

Jeff finished telling Martin about his night and realized his whole body had tensed up. He was angry all over again.

"I know Siena might be feeling all kinds of pain, but I can't quite find a way to hold onto that story. I keep coming back to how no one has kids like this. People talk about how their kids are so easy or are such good sleepers, and I want to strangle them. Then I think about Yvette, and it's the same thing. I handed in my performance review yesterday. She seemed to be in a good mood. No problem, right? I'm seeing like a hero, but I don't know how long I will be able to keep that up if she keeps criticizing me forever."

Jeff's frustration was spilling out of him. Martin pointed toward the door. "Do you have time to take a walk? I think now would be a good time for you to hear about the second kind of story."

Situation Stories

The Park

It was cool outside, but the fresh air felt good. Martin led Jeff out of the building and a couple of blocks away to a nearby park. Jeff wondered why he didn't do this more often. He could feel his head clearing. Just this short walk, the fresh air, the trees in the park were relieving some of his tension.

They stopped at a railing that bordered a pond. Martin leaned against the railing and stared out at the water. Jeff could see him taking long deep breaths. It was almost hypnotic.

They stood in silence for a while until Jeff's impatience got the better of him. "So what is the next story?"

"First, tell me what you see."

"You mean here in the park?"

Martin nodded.

"I see a pond, trees, building tops beyond the trees. There are lots of birds, mostly pigeons, a few ducks."

"That's good. How about the people?"

Jeff looked around. "Well, a young couple is sitting on the bench over there. Some old men are playing bocce. A handful of people are scattered around — I assume from the way they are dressed that they are businesspeople."

"Tell me about these people. What is their story?"

Jeff looked at the couple on the bench, smiling at each other, laughing occasionally. The old men were having fun with their game. The businesspeople were talking on cell phones, reading books or papers, or simply walking through the park.

"They all look pretty relaxed. I mean, they're spending time in a park. They look like they are right where they want to be."

"Very good. Now if I told you some of them spend time here every day—being right where they want to be every single day—would you envy them?"

Jeff thought about how it would feel to have that kind of freedom. It had been a long time since he had last been in a place he would describe as right where he wanted to be. "I sure would. Some people live very fortunate lives. I'd love to be able to do what I wanted to do every day."

"I think we all would. Now tell me about the people we saw on our way to the park."

Jeff had a difficult time remembering anyone. They were all just a blur of pedestrians. "I don't know. I guess there were shoppers and businesspeople."

"Tell me their story."

Jeff had to use his imagination for this since he barely remembered anyone they passed, but he gave it a shot.

"OK. They are busy. They're moving. They just want to get where they are going."

"Are they happy?" Martin asked in response.

"Some yes, some no. But that's not what they're about. The people here in the park are all about being happy and relaxed. The people on the street are going somewhere. They are all about moving and doing."

"OK, same question. If I told you some of them are like that all the time. They move and do things. They are focused on being productive. Would you envy them?"

Jeff felt that was a pretty accurate picture of his own life. He helps with Siena in the morning. Then he's off to work, where he has to focus all day on being productive, moving, doing. Then he goes home and has to cook dinner or watch Siena while Marie cooks dinner. Then it's the bedtime routine, falling asleep exhausted, and sometimes doing the nightshift with Siena.

"It's hard to say. I love to be productive and create things and do good work, but sometimes I need downtime. This 24/7 productivity is where I am right now and it's brutal. All I want is a break. Frankly, I'd bet the people we passed on the sidewalk probably get a lot more relaxation time than I do."

"It doesn't sound like you are in a very enviable position right now."

"It sure doesn't feel that—" Jeff stopped short. He saw Martin was smiling. He suddenly realized what Martin was about to say.

"That's the second story isn't it? I was just telling a story about what it was like to be me."

"That's right," Martin said. "You were the victim of your circumstances. The first story is the story you tell about other people. The second story is the story you tell about your situation, and just like the first story, it can be that of either a hero or a victim."

It had been so easy for Jeff to construct stories in which everyone around him had it better than he did. They had more freedom and relaxation and better lives. It was shocking how quickly the stories had come to him.

Martin continued, "The stories we tell about our situations are often about what we don't have. When you want something and see that others have it, you can feel envious. You don't have time to relax. You don't get to go to the park. You don't get to sit quietly on a bench with your wife and smile and laugh.

"Those are your places of envy right now. They are where you see the world from a victim viewpoint, but other people focus on other areas. They might look at someone else's clothes or car or job. I guarantee you that other people have stood in this exact spot, leaned against this rail, looked up at the tops of those buildings, and felt frustrated and angry that those penthouses didn't belong to them.

"Then there are some of the most personal envies of all. These are the types of envy in which a person begins to wish for different parents or friends, a different spouse or different children."

As Martin said this, a breeze blew some leaves past Jeff's legs. They swirled, climbed into the air, and dove before finally settling on the path a few yards away. Jeff looked at these leaves blowing by and thought about the regrets, disappointments, and frustrations he had felt lately.

He couldn't even count the number of times he had felt envy over other people's kids. He wouldn't give up Siena for anything, but he knew many times he had looked longingly at other kids, who seemed so calm, quiet, and easy.

"So the stories I've been telling are that I've got a tough kid, I don't have any time for myself, and I've got a boss who just wants to beat me up."

"That sounds about right," said Martin.

Jeff thought there was a problem with this. "For the stories about other people, you said the truth wasn't that important because it was often impossible to tell. If two stories are equally likely to be true or untrue, the hero chooses the one that makes him happier and more effective. The victim chooses the one that leaves him angry and frustrated."

"That's right."

"But I know the story of my situation. It is true I have a tough kid. I don't have time for myself. I do have a boss who is very critical of me. Those things are all true. I can't just pretend those things don't exist."

"No?"

Jeff could tell Martin was going to challenge his thinking, so he figured he might as well dive right in.

"OK, so what's the question that is supposed to turn these stories around?"

"I'll be happy to tell you, but first you need to see something else."

74

The Hospital

Martin pushed himself away from the rail and took one last long look around. As he finished perusing the scenery he said, "One thing you should know is what you choose to see matters a great deal."

With that he turned and began to walk down a new path leading out of the park. Jeff hurried to keep up and tried to absorb Martin's last words. He looked around at the scenery. He wanted to enjoy his last few moments of time in the park, but he kept thinking about the stories of envy.

He looked at the people they passed — men and women, old and young, some well-dressed, others not. Nothing struck him one way or another.

Then they were out of the park, and Martin was leading him down streets that were unfamiliar. They were fewer than ten blocks from his office, but this was a direction Jeff just didn't travel.

The people were a little younger and a little less well dressed. Then Jeff saw a couple of homeless people, and he assumed he understood the lesson. He was so intent on his thoughts, he didn't notice when Martin stopped walking, and he nearly bumped into him.

"I've got it Martin. I understand. In the park we saw people who have a lot more than I have. If we keep going further north from here, the neighborhood gets a lot poorer. We've already passed a couple of homeless people. There are people in this world who don't have a lot. If I think about them, I'll feel better about my own situation."

Martin nodded his head. "That's part of it. You can think about the story of your situation in two ways. You just described the first, which is about looking outward. When you look outward you compare yourself to others. You have either a pretty good life or a pretty poor life, depending on which direction you look. Back at the park we could look up at the penthouse apartments. When we look in that direction we will feel frustrated with our lives. Here, just a few blocks away, we can look at homeless people. That comparison will make us feel fairly fortunate."

"OK," Jeff said. "I understand the idea, but can I challenge you?"

"I'd be disappointed if you held back. What's up?"

"It's just this feels a little Pollyanna to me. I mean, am I supposed to be happy because I'm not homeless? It reminds me of my mother telling me to be happy I had Brussels sprouts because there were starving people in the world."

"Hey, I like Brussels sprouts," Martin said with a mock hurt tone, "but I understand what you're saying. Comparing yourself to others to see how fortunate you are works for some situations and not for others. I also find that for me it helps for the comparison to be closer to home. Starving people on the other side of the planet may not be as meaningful as a homeless person you pass on the street every day. And that homeless person won't be as meaningful as the one you meet and speak with when you volunteer at a local soup kitchen."

Jeff thought about the times when he had volunteered in his life. "You know, it's true that when I have done volunteer work with people less fortunate than I am, afterward I have generally been much more appreciative of what I have. Then that feeling fades, and I find myself thinking more about the penthouses."

"It's easy," Martin said, "to tell the story that other people have so much more than you do, unless you practice telling yourself a different story. And the more specific your story is, the more it will help you refocus. In my own case, there is a very specific story that reminds me to be thankful for what I have."

Martin looked across the street, and Jeff followed his gaze. He was looking at a hospital. As is usually the case, a number of people were walking in or out of the building — doctors, nurses, patients. It was a standard urban hospital.

Jeff was about to speak, but something in the way Martin looked stopped him. Instead, he watched the hospital and waited for Martin to speak. Eventually, he did.

"Five years ago my niece was born. She was a beautiful baby. My brother, Ed, was already out of college when you got to high school, so you probably don't remember him. He was as proud as could be. After three boys, this was his first girl. I mean, he and his wife radiated pure joy. I was there at the hospital with them. It could have been this one or any other hospital across the country. I was physically there, but I wasn't really with them. Three weeks earlier my son had been diagnosed with diabetes."

Jeff was taken aback by this. He wanted to say something supportive, but Martin was deep inside his story, so Jeff let him continue.

"I couldn't believe it, couldn't accept it. I was shocked and furious and terrified. I had been given all the news: it was a life-long disease — he'd never be rid of it. We'd have to give him daily shots until he was old enough to give them to himself. We'd have to monitor his blood sugar levels. If he went without his insulin shots for an extended period, it could be fatal.

"There was good news too. Diabetics can live long and happy lives. With advances in monitoring and administration, it is less of a threat, even less of an inconvenience. But I couldn't hear any of that. I was angry all day and all night.

"When my niece was born I made a brief appearance in the room, said congratulations, and then made an excuse about being hungry so I could get away. I went down to the hospital cafeteria and got a cup of lousy, burned coffee. The cafeteria was pretty busy at the time, so I had to share a table with someone.

"Well, this guy I sat down with looked the way I felt. That was fine with me. I was angry at the world. My perfect son had been taken away from me. I had to stick needles into him every day. My life was miserable. If someone else felt the same way I did, so be it.

"At first I didn't say anything, but I did steal a few glances at him. The more I looked at him, the worse he looked. Eventually, I became convinced that as bad as I felt, this guy felt worse, much worse. I knew I was angry. This guy looked like his soul was being eaten away.

"I couldn't believe I was actually doing this, but I spoke. I asked him if he was OK. He looked up at me, and I can't begin to describe the depth of pain I saw in his eyes.

"We got to talking and he told me his story. He was there because his son was a patient in the neurological unit. His son was fourteen months old and was having seizures. They had started recently and were now coming repeatedly throughout the day.

"The doctors were trying to figure out why the seizures were happening and how they could be stopped. The 'good' options included some pretty heavy steroids. The bad option was brain surgery.

"Over the next three years, the family tried pretty much every option to cure the seizures. They tried the steroid treatments. Their kid went through three brain surgeries, by the end of which they had removed almost the entire right side of his brain.

"They celebrated things like the day he was three years old and used a sippy cup all by himself for the first time. They celebrated when the seizures had been reduced to only a handful per day. And when they finally decided things were going well enough for them to cancel plans for another surgery, that same week this man's wife was diagnosed with breast cancer."

Martin stopped talking. He looked drained, and Jeff didn't know what to say. After a while he simply said, "I'm sorry."

"So am I," Martin replied. "Although I'm also thankful he came into my life. See, I use his story to draw inspiration from how strong he has been. This is what I mean by the power of a specific story. Starving people on the other side of the world don't help me keep perspective. A person like my friend, who I know personally, is a much stronger reminder. Thinking of him reminds me to appreciate what I have, and he inspires me to tell heroic stories no matter what challenge I face."

Martin's point was interrupted by the blare of sirens as an ambulance drove down the block and pulled into the emergency room driveway. Jeff and Martin watched the ambulance stop and the paramedics jump out, pull a stretcher from the back, and roll it into the hospital.

Jeff was the first to speak after witnessing this scene. "So even remembering what we just saw isn't enough? I need to remember something more specific?"

"The more specific you can be," Martin replied, "the more your new story will help you. When I remember my friend, it snaps me back to a more positive and appreciative frame of mind. Tragedies occur every day. They are all around us. We think of luck and we look at things like the lottery and getting the right jobs, catching our morning train or getting the last blueberry muffin. These things are all irrelevant when you look at the challenges or even tragedies some people suffer."

Jeff looked up at the hospital and thought about the hundreds of rooms inside, some filled with heartache, some filled with joy. Then he remembered something Martin had said earlier.

"Didn't you say there were two ways to think about your situation?"

"That's right," Martin said. "We've been talking about looking outward — comparing yourself with others. The victim always compares himself with people who have more. The hero sees how many people have less. That's the outward comparison. You can also change the way you look inward. Looking inward is about which aspects of your life you choose to focus on. Come on."

As he finished his sentence, Martin stepped out into the crosswalk. Jeff followed him as he crossed the street and walked over to the front of the hospital. Large windows revealed a lobby area with people walking through or taking advantage of the seating provided.

"Look at the people in there. Any one of the unhappy-looking ones could have been me when I visited my brother."

Jeff looked at the crowd and found a woman sitting on a bench. Leaning against her and apparently asleep was a child who looked about eight years old. The woman, who was dressed in typical urban-chic clothes and was probably in her midthirties, looked like she might also fall asleep at any time. Many other people wore similar expressions of exhaustion, and most wore scowls as well.

Looking through the window, Martin asked, "Where was I focusing my attention?"

"On your son," Jeff answered.

"That's right. All of my attention was on my son. I failed to focus on the birth of my niece, a happy and uplifting event in my life. What I didn't tell you about that time was I had also just started my coaching business. Things went well from the beginning. It was one of the most exciting things I had ever done in my life. I had an amazingly strong wife who could tackle any challenge and was ready to deal with whatever our son's diabetes threw our way. I had friends, family, rewarding work, and a good home. So why didn't I focus on any of that?"

The answer was obvious, Jeff thought. "How could you? Your son was in trouble."

Martin stared at him until Jeff couldn't take it anymore.

"You're not going to tell me you should have ignored your son's situation. This is crazy. Why shouldn't you have focused all of your attention on —"

Jeff halted in midsentence as he suddenly thought he saw the answer. It came back to the same issue they had discussed the day before. The story Martin had told made him angry and ineffective. Why keep telling the story if that's what it does?

"OK," Jeff said. "Now I'm confused. I think I see what's happening. Your story, in this case your focus, was centered on what was going wrong in your life. If you shifted your focus to the good things in your life, you would be happier and more effective. Is that right so far?"

Martin nodded his head.

"Then I still have a question. Does this mean I'm supposed to try to ignore what's going wrong?"

"Not at all," Martin said. "It just means that if you spend all of your time focused on what is wrong, you'll make yourself miserable. Thinking about and appreciating the good things in your life gives you a counterbalance that lifts your spirits and makes you better able to respond effectively to the challenges. My wife didn't ignore our son's diabetes, but she didn't make herself into a victim because of it. As a result, she ended up with much more strength than I had to deal with the situation."

Jeff could see that on the day Martin's niece was born he chose a story that caused him to wallow in his sadness instead of choosing a story that would allow him to be happy and able to celebrate with his family.

Martin continued, "When you look at your situation you can look outward or inward. When you look outward you have a choice between looking at those who have everything you want or those who have none of what you have. When you look inward you have a choice between looking at the worst elements in your life or the best. So the question to change your story about your situation is actually the same as the question you ask to change stories about other people: what would the hero see?"

Situation Stories

Victims tell stories that focus on the worst
elements in their lives.
Ask, **what would the hero see?**
to connect you with what is positive in your life.

Jeff thought about this for a moment. "So when you're upset about your situation, you should ask yourself what the hero would see?"

"That's right. Think about it. The hero is the one in the story who has the attitude that whatever just happened wasn't so bad. Victims always believe the world is falling apart around them. Think about my situation. What was I choosing to see when I was so upset?"

Jeff thought about what Martin had said earlier in the park. We see the things we don't have and tell stories based on those things.

"I guess you were probably looking at everyone who still had what you thought of as perfect kids. Your brother was just the most recent reminder for you that your son wasn't perfect."

"OK. So my story was that I had a terrible situation. My son wasn't perfect, and everyone around me had perfect kids. Where wasn't I looking?"

The story Martin had told about the man he met in the cafeteria was a pretty stark contrast. Jeff couldn't imagine the pain and struggle of dealing with that kind of challenge, especially with his child.

"Well, you weren't looking at people like your friend from the hospital."

"True. I failed to look at him or people like him. That was my failure when I looked outward. What did I fail to see when I looked inward?"

"Well, I don't want to minimize the pain or challenge you experienced, but I have a friend with diabetes. He seems to live a pretty full life. In fact, he's more adventurous, more active, and more successful than I am. You still had a pretty terrific child, not to mention a new niece, a strong wife, and an exciting new business."

"You got it," Martin said. "The lesson here isn't to ignore the issues in your life, but you don't have to wallow in them either.

Now let me share one more piece of my friend's story—the part that inspires me the most. Through all of the challenges he and his wife have faced, they have told the most heroic stories I have ever heard.

"They point out how supportive their family and friends have been during their ordeals, how wonderful their doctors are, and how well they as a family persevered through all of it. They talk about hospital waiting rooms in which they have met people facing tougher challenges than their own.

"In the depths of tremendously painful health crises that affected their whole family on a daily basis, what did they see? They saw all of the wonderful things they had."

Jeff was amazed. "Wow. They sound like incredible people. I don't think I would be able to do that."

"I agree that they are incredible people. I disagree that you wouldn't be able to do it. You just need to know where to look. When you only look at what you don't have and what's wrong in your life, your story is always that of the victim. You need to learn to see people who are less fortunate than you are and also to see how much you have. Then you will see like a hero."

Together they began walking back toward Jeff's building. On the walk back Jeff thought about his own situation. He wasn't rich, but he had a good job that paid a pretty decent salary. He owned his house with a reasonable mortgage and was able to make most purchases without worrying about money. He was married to a wonderful woman and had a baby who cried a lot but was basically healthy.

Lately his stories had all been about his crying baby, the fights with his wife, and his critical boss, but these stories were making him miserable and ineffective. Thinking about how much he loved his wife and daughter made him feel more eager to help them. Thinking about how Yvette had helped the careers of the previous people who had held his position made him want to work harder.

As they walked he said to Martin, "I guess I am pretty lucky. I mean, I may not be able to buy everything I want, but I've got a good job. I've got a basically healthy family. I've got plenty of good friends who would help me if I was in need. Life is pretty good."

"Actually, life is even better than you think." Martin stopped walking and the other pedestrians flowed around them on the sidewalk. "Sure, we have wealth and health. We have friends and family. We also have freedom and opportunity. How many people on this planet are born with the rights, the safety and security, or the possibilities we were given just by being born where we were?"

Jeff looked around the busy city street. On this block were a couple of restaurants and a handful of shops, including a bookstore and some clothing stores. The pedestrians — businesspeople and shoppers, typical for this area — were going in and out of stores or simply walking along.

He thought about his own upbringing in a middle-class family. Then he thought about countries ravaged by war, poverty, famine, and disease. He looked through the window of a restaurant and watched the people inside. There was nothing unusual about the scene. Yet somehow the normalcy of it made Jeff realize how much he took for granted — his job, a loving wife, a healthy child, a good home, and so much more.

"I do have quite a lot," he said. "But now I need to challenge you again. Where I was born will never change. Yes, I was lucky to have been born with these freedoms and opportunities. Does this mean that for my whole life I never have the right to be angry or sad?"

"That," Martin said, "is a very interesting way to phrase your question."

Jeff looked puzzled.

"You asked if you have the 'right' to be angry or sad. I would suggest you have the right to feel anything you want. To me the real question is, how is your anger or your sadness working for you?"

Jeff still looked confused. "How is it working for me?"

"Yes. Does it lead you in a direction you want to go? Does it make you feel the way you want to feel? Does it lead to outcomes you desire?"

Jeff paused as he considered this. "Well, I certainly don't enjoy feeling angry or sad. Most of the time when I feel that way I am not motivated. I make bad decisions. I'm not very considerate. I guess it's not working very well for me."

Martin smiled. "Once again, you have the right to feel any way you want. That means when things go poorly, you have the right to feel angry. It also means at those very same times, you have the right to feel grateful and even happy. You will undoubtedly encounter situations in your life that make you angry or sad. Now you simply know you don't have to stay angry or sad. You can choose to see like a hero and tell a new story that works better for you."

As they walked on in silence, Jeff thought about some of his colleagues from the Fast Track program. When they were rotating through the company, they used to meet occasionally to share their experiences. They had all worked in a variety of departments and for a variety of bosses. One would think they would all have had a mix of good and bad experiences. Yet some of them felt every manager was lousy and every assignment was somehow lacking.

Others drew very different conclusions. They learned a lot from this manager or from that assignment. They saw opportunities in each rotation. They were more excited about their past positions and the possibilities of their future jobs.

As a manager, Jeff realized there was no question which group he would rather have on his team. While Jeff mulled over these differences, they arrived back at his office building. Martin hailed a cab and as it pulled up, he turned back to Jeff.

"Remember, when you ask what the hero would see, the purpose is to tell a story of your good fortune. When you do this, you build your ability to feel gratitude. We all have much to be grateful for, but we frequently lose track of those things. Gratitude is the second strength that will guide you to greater happiness and success."

> Heroic stories about your situation build gratitude.

Jeff was disappointed to see his time with Martin end, but he knew they both had to get back to work.

"Martin, I'm grateful right now for everything you've shared, and I still want to ask for more. I want to hear about the third story. Will you be able to share it?"

Martin smiled. "You're lucky I'm here all week. Tomorrow meet me again for lunch, twelve thirty."

Living on the Beach

Jeff went back to work with his situation stories bouncing around in his head. He thought about his family and how lucky he was. The way he felt in that moment, he couldn't believe he had ever felt otherwise.

Then his mind turned to his job. It was a pretty good job. He was advancing in his career. Yes, he was having some issues with his boss, but overall he thought she still supported him.

Jeff was snapped out of his reverie by his phone ringing. He looked at the caller ID and saw his friend Art's number flash up.

Jeff picked up the receiver and said, "What's happening?"

Art's cheerful voice on the other end responded, "Still living on the beach."

Art had been laid off from his job three months prior and liked to refer to his current situation that way. He said he liked how the beach created an image of relaxation. Jeff had never been comfortable with the term before. He had been angry at Art's company even while Art wasn't angry himself. Now Jeff thought maybe he understood.

"Art, I need to ask you a question about the beach."

"If you want to know if there's space on the beach for you, the answer is always yes. But I think you, my friend, are better off in the A/C."

That was another one of Art's phrases. He referred to the corporate world as living in the A/C for air conditioning.

"That's kind of what I wanted to ask you about. Why are you so happy about living on the beach? Actually, I don't want to ask it that way. You're not on a beach. You were laid off. You lost your job. I don't want to be mean, but that's the truth. Why are you so happy about it?"

"Hmm, it seems like my friend is having a deep-thought kind of day. What's going on over there?"

Jeff smiled. Underneath his blasé exterior Art was very perceptive. It could catch him off-guard at times. "You're right. I am having deep thoughts, and I'll tell you all about them. But first I want you to answer my question."

"OK, do you remember when Hayley lost her job?"

Hayley had lived in the apartment next door to Art and Jeff when they first moved to the city after their trip to Europe.

"Sure. It'd be hard to forget the tirade she went on that night. In fact, I think she was still fuming a year later."

"That's right. And how long did it take her to find a new job?"

"About six months."

"And what's the worst thing that happened to her in those six months," Art asked.

"I don't know what the worst thing was. I'm sure it was embarrassing and frightening for her. I remember we took that big trip down to New Orleans for the jazz festival. She was pretty upset she couldn't go, but she didn't feel she could afford it."

Jeff heard Art laughing on the other end. "I do remember that trip. My favorite part was you ordering the superspicy jambalaya and then complaining that your mouth was burning for the next three hours."

"Yes, yes," Jeff said. "Stay focused here. You were talking about Hayley."

"Right. So what is her job like now?"

"She has a great job. She ended up switching out of finance and into advertising, and she says she loves it."

"Exactly," Art said.

"Exactly what? Hayley was furious when she was fired. You have always seemed happy you were laid off. I want to understand why."

"Well, I think you've missed my meaning. I've never been happy I was laid off. Getting laid off is a lousy experience, but it's not the end of the world. We've both known people who have lost their jobs. Nothing terrible happened to any of them. None of them are roaming the streets today. Even Amy's friend Lucas — remember him?"

"Sure," said Jeff.

Lucas had lost his job and had to move out of his apartment as a result. He stayed with some friends for awhile. Then he got another job and found a new apartment and life went on.

"I'm not happy I was laid off," Art said, "and I'm working as hard as I can to find a new job. I'm just not willing to be miserable in the process. I don't think it does any good. In fact, when I look at Hayley, I think it made things worse for her. She was a nervous wreck before all of her interviews. She was snippy with her friends, and she missed out on being happy for six months. So, does that answer your question, my corporate friend?"

"Art, as always, you've shown me the light, and now one of us has to get back to work."

"Hey!" Art called out. "I thought you were going to tell me about your deep thoughts."

"Tomorrow. In fact, I think I'll have more to tell then anyway. Be good."

"Never," Art replied.

Jeff hung up the phone and laughed. All this time his best friend had been telling the stories he had just learned. If he had paid better attention, he might have learned this from Art a long time ago.

He wondered if Art knew all three stories and looked forward to hearing the third story the following day.

Self Stories

Special Treats

The next day Jeff arrived in the lobby at precisely twelve thirty. This time Martin was standing alone. When he walked up, Martin grabbed him by the shoulders.

"Today, my friend, I have two very special treats in store for you. The first is that I am going to introduce you to one of my favorite people. She'll be joining us at lunch, and we don't want to keep her waiting. So let's go."

A part of Jeff was annoyed by this. It was petty, but he wanted Martin's time to himself. He had gotten so much out of the last two days he didn't want anything to spoil his opportunity to learn the third story.

Then Jeff realized what he had done. In only an instant he had made himself into a victim. His situation wasn't what he wanted. Woe is me. He nearly laughed out loud. The hero would see the opportunity in this situation. He got to have lunch with not one, but two wonderful people.

Martin ushered Jeff outside and into a cab. After Martin gave the driver an address they both watched the city glide by for a few minutes. Then Martin turned to Jeff and asked, "So? Any more revelations for me?"

"Actually, yes."

Jeff recounted his experience with Art the day before and Martin nodded his approval.

"Is Art Jackie's little brother," Martin asked.

"One and the same."

"I should have known you two would still be friends. You were always together in high school if I remember."

"We were pretty close back then. Still are."

"Well Art sounds like a good friend to have around to keep you grounded."

"I guess he is," Jeff said. "I always thought I was the one who grounded him. I'm more of a realist. I play things a little safer than he does, but you're right. In many ways he helps me see what's important in life. And speaking of what's important, didn't you mention you had two treats for me today?"

Martin smiled. As if on cue, the cab stopped. Martin paid the driver and they got out. They were standing in the middle of a block that looked residential. There were no storefronts, no awnings. In front of them was a building devoid of any identifying markings other than a small sign that read Pauvre Diable. In smaller lettering underneath was the translation: "poor devil." Anyone who didn't already know there was a restaurant here would walk by without noticing.

"Here is the second treat. The chef here used to work in the kitchen at the restaurant where I worked as a host in college. I think you'll enjoy this."

Martin led him inside to a completely unexpected room. The outside may have looked like a place everyone would pass by, but clearly lots of people knew to stop. The place was packed. The decor was elegant but comfortable, upscale but not pretentious: paintings on the walls by local artists, a bar with plush couches for seating, and a wait staff who seemingly had everything under complete control.

When the hostess saw Martin, she walked over to greet him with a kiss on each cheek. Clearly he was known here as well.

As the hostess guided them to a table Jeff asked Martin, "Do you get this treatment at every restaurant in town?"

Martin smiled. "Not every one. But I do try to make friends wherever I go."

The table was at the back of the restaurant in a quiet corner next to the kitchen. On the table a small vase of pink and white lilies gave off a subtle but beautiful aroma that mingled with the scents emanating from the kitchen.

When they were seated, the hostess offered them each a menu and then disappeared. They made small talk while looking over the menus. Jeff learned that Martin had helped the chef hire the staff, and the hostess was an aspiring actress. He also discovered that everything on the menu at Pauvre Diable sounded delicious.

When the waiter came to take their order, Jeff told him they were waiting for a third, but Martin suggested they go ahead and order.

Jeff opted for the comfort of steak frites — a simple grilled steak with French fries — while Martin ordered the duck.

Once their orders were placed Martin said, "All right. Now it's time to see if you are ready for the third story."

"Ready?" Jeff asked.

"Yes. Before you learn the third story, it is important you clearly understand the first two stories. Humor me. Tell me what you've already learned."

Jeff felt some pressure to show Martin he had paid attention. "OK," he began, "first I learned we all tell ourselves stories that make us into either heroes or victims. On Monday I learned about stories I tell about people. When I get angry with other people, it is usually because of the stories I tell about them, not necessarily about what they did. My stories blame them or make them out to be inconsiderate or mean people."

"That's good," Martin said. "So what do you do about it?"

"I tell a new story. I ask myself, what would the hero see? That question helps me to see their challenges or pain and to build the strength of empathy. When I feel for them, I am more willing to listen and more eager to help. In the end, seeing their pain improves my relationships and makes me happier and more successful."

"Very good. You've been doing your homework."

"I'm just beginning to learn how to tell hero stories," Jeff said.

"All right. What else?"

"Yesterday I learned about stories I tell about my situation. Even if I can empathize with other people, that doesn't take away the fact that I will experience tough situations. When I focus on my difficulties and what isn't working in my life, I get frustrated. I also tend to notice people who are better off than I am — have a better job or relationship, more money, or easier kids. Focusing on such people makes me feel worse about my situation, and my stories in turn grow even worse."

Martin was nodding along.

Jeff continued, "Instead, I need to again ask, what would the hero see? That turns my attention to the positive things in my life. It helps me remember to look at how many people in the world aren't as fortunate as I am. It reminds me not to take for granted what I have. All of this builds the strength of gratitude."

Jeff sat back and thought about what he had just explained. He was amazed at how simple yet effective these stories were. Still, there was something that didn't seem right in all of this.

Jasmin

The soothing music softly playing in the background seemed perfectly in line with the serenity that resulted from Martin's stories. On Monday morning Jeff would have sworn he had a mean boss and a miserable family situation, and that he was living a tough life. Now he felt great. He believed his boss, his wife, and his daughter were all doing their best and that he had a pretty darned good life, but he still had a significant doubt about the value of the stories he had learned to tell.

Jeff leaned forward in his chair and said, "I don't understand where the people and situation stories leave me. I feel better now than I have in a long time about myself, my life, and the people around me. Still, I can't help wondering how long this feeling will last. I mean, these stories seem to suggest I just need to accept everything. That doesn't seem right."

"OK, I'm convinced. You're ready for the third story. First, I have to make an observation."

"What's that?" asked Jeff, concerned.

"You really seem to like asking challenging questions."

Jeff was afraid he had said something wrong, but Martin broke into a wide grin and said, "We have a saying at my company: 'To question is to learn. To doubt is normal. To challenge is to share your soul.' When someone questions what we teach, it means they are on the path to changing their beliefs or ours. Either outcome is good. Now I hope I can help you finish this journey."

Jeff felt a little in over his head, but he mumbled that he hoped so, too.

Martin smiled. "So you clearly know about the first two stories. Remind me what you were saying a minute ago. You had some concern?"

"Yeah. It seems with the first two stories I'm just supposed to accept things in my life even if they are lousy. If my boss criticizes me, I should see her pain. If my kid is tough, I should appreciate what I have. Doesn't this make it so I just have to take whatever comes my way?"

Martin nodded his head through everything Jeff said. "That's exactly how a lot of people feel when they get through the first two stories about people and situations. They don't want to just sit back and wait for life to change. Then they learn the third story, and it all makes sense."

"Well, I'm ready. Tell me the story."

"First, it's important to better understand what the first two stories do for you, because without them, the third story becomes very difficult to tell."

Jeff was eager to hear how the three stories fit together. In fact, he was so eager he didn't even notice someone had walked up and was standing behind him.

"I believe this is where I come in," said a voice over Jeff's shoulder.

He turned to see a tall woman in a chef's uniform. Martin got up immediately and the two hugged.

"Jasmin, get back in the kitchen," said Martin playfully. "I want you to be the one cooking my duck."

"Yes," replied the woman, "but if I always cook, how will they learn? And who better for them to make a mistake on than you?"

"Some things never change," said Martin with a laugh. Then he turned to the table. "Jeff, this is Jasmin. She is the chef and owner of Pauvre Diable and a good friend when she isn't insulting me."

Jasmin laughed and turned to the table. "Jeff, it is a pleasure to meet you. Welcome to my home away from home."

"You've built a fantastic place here," said Jeff.

"And that," added Martin, "comes from a guy who hasn't even eaten your cooking yet."

"Well, there will be time for that," said Jasmin. "It sounded like you were about to discuss the third story. True?"

"That's right," answered Martin.

"Wow. Does everyone you know live by these stories?" Jeff asked.

Jasmin jumped in before Martin could respond. "You can't stop him from telling people about them, but they are great stories. So, I overheard you were about to explain the value of the first two stories. Shall I tell my own story?"

"I was hoping you would," replied Martin.

That was how Jeff wound up alongside Martin and Jasmin,

standing against a wall in the kitchen of Pauvre Diable during the lunchtime rush. Jasmin had led them in to see a half dozen chefs at work, preparing sauces, cutting, chopping, baking, grilling, all of them working in complete harmony.

Jeff had looked into the kitchen at the Italian restaurant on Monday, but this kitchen was different. The chefs here seemed more precise, more focused. But one thing was the same: the food smelled delicious.

Jasmin began to speak. "At the first restaurant I worked in coming out of culinary school, the head chef was angry all the time. He barked at me if there was the slightest imperfection in any of my preparations. He did this even if it was because of something out of my control. Look at these asparagus."

Jasmin grabbed a handful of asparagus from a container on one of the counters. "What's wrong with them?" she asked.

She looked to Jeff to answer. The asparagus were all cut to the same length, all approximately the same width. Jeff didn't want to criticize Jasmin's food, but even if he wanted to be critical, the asparagus looked perfectly normal to him.

"I don't know," he said. "Nothing?"

"I remember one time," Jasmin said, "my boss yelled at me for serving asparagus just like this. He said they were too thick. Perhaps he was right, but I wasn't responsible for buying the asparagus. Still, he yelled at me all the same. I was barely being paid a living wage. I had no social life because I was always working when other people with normal lives were going out. I didn't need his abuse. So what stories do you think I told? And remember, this was before Martin's epiphany of the three stories was revealed to me."

At the sauté station a pan suddenly flared up as one of the chefs added some wine. The chef's face glowed orange for a few seconds while the alcohol in the wine burned off. At the same time, two other chefs were working together to arrange polenta, Cornish hens, and spinach on a pair of plates.

Jeff glanced over to see Martin and Jasmin had wide grins on their faces. Clearly they loved the drama of the kitchen and were witnessing a great team at work here. It reminded him of the best working situations of his life — the camaraderie, the teamwork. Then he thought about Jasmin's prior job, and he could relate to much of what she was saying.

"Well, you probably thought your boss was a tyrant," Jeff said. "I'm sure you were pretty angry at him most of the time. As for your situation, maybe you started to generalize: I'll always be poor; I'll never have time to date or see my friends."

Jasmin nodded her head. "I told all of those stories and went one step farther with regard to my situation. I convinced myself I had chosen the wrong profession, that I had taken the wrong life path. Can you imagine? After years of schooling and dreaming, I was finally where I had always wanted to be, and I thought I had made a mistake."

"Wow," Jeff responded, "that must have been tough to bear."

"It sure was. Now here comes the important question that brings us to our third story. What did I do about it?"

Jeff gave her a blank stare. "What did you do?"

"That's right," Jasmin said. "What did I do? I had all this frustration, anger, even a little depression. What did I do?"

"I don't know. You've got this restaurant. So I guess you looked for and found a new job."

"Not even close," Jasmin replied. "I wallowed."

"You wallowed?"

"That's right. I wallowed. I went to work every day and hated my boss. I went out for drinks after work with the other people who hated him. I avoided seeing my friends because they all had such wonderful lives to talk about. I even made some mistakes in the kitchen on purpose when I thought my boss wouldn't catch them."

Jeff was surprised. "What kinds of mistakes did you make?"

"I oversalted, I undercooked, and other little things that got past the head chef but probably lowered the customers' views of the restaurant."

"Wow," Jeff said again.

Suddenly Jasmin dashed off to a chef who was taking a steak out of the broiler. She said something to the chef, who nodded in response, and then Jasmin returned.

Martin chided her: "Hey, let them cook. If they don't cook, they won't learn."

"And you, my old friend, never learn," Jasmin responded with a smile. "Your food is almost ready. Let's head back to the table."

Then she ushered them out of the kitchen and to their table.

"Let me be clear here," she said once they were all seated. "I am not proud of these actions. They were the wrong things to do. I had convinced myself my situation was terrible. I was in the wrong career. I worked for an ogre. My stories made me miserable, and they made me do a lot of things I regret. Then there was the date."

"You mean you went out on a date?" Jeff asked.

"I sure did—kicking and screaming. One of my friends set me up, and I can assure you she hasn't even considered doing so again. I made sure of that."

"What did you do?"

"This poor guy took me out to eat at a nice French restaurant named Ti Pa, which is short for 'little father.' It was a cute place. My date was nice. He was even good looking. Well, early on he said something to me about how much he loved his work, and from then on I had it in for him. I returned my dinner three times. I criticized the decor of the restaurant. I complained about my life. I was probably the worst date he ever had. And why do you suppose that was?"

Jeff knew the routine by now. "Was it because of your stories?"

"You got it. So let's go back to what this means about the first two stories. How did my old stories make me act?"

"You became angry," Jeff answered, "and bitter and mean. You sabotaged yourself."

"Yes," Jasmin responded. "And the amazing thing is if you had pointed this out to me, I would have looked at you as though you had two heads. I thought the guy from the blind date was a jerk because he didn't want to go out with me again. I thought all of my actions were justified.

"Now let's look at a new scenario. What if I had been telling better stories? Had I seen my boss through a hero's eyes, I would have realized a bunch of things. The economy was slumping. People weren't going out to restaurants that much. My boss was watching his business lose money and possibly head into bankruptcy.

"Meanwhile, I wasn't the first person in the world with a bad boss. And I wasn't the first person to question my career choice. So what? You know from the second story that lots of situations in the world were a lot worse than mine, and that I probably had plenty of good things in my life as well."

Jeff was concerned they were back where they started. "So, once again, you could have been happier with better stories. But doesn't this still leave you just accepting your situation?" Jasmin smiled. "Now we are truly at the third story."

The Third Story Is Served

From the kitchen came two waiters carrying plates of food to their table. Martin's duck was pink inside with a crispy bronze skin, cooked to perfection. And Jeff's steak frites was exactly as he expected it to be, with the addition of a side of asparagus with some kind of mushroom on top.

Jasmin smiled at Jeff's inquisitive look. "These are asparagus with morel mushrooms and a drizzle of truffle butter for you, compliments of the house. After all, a hero tries new things."

With that, Jasmin winked at him and disappeared back into the kitchen. Jeff watched her walk away, then turned back to the table to find Martin already with fork and knife in hand, exploring his food with a rapturous look on his face.

Jeff decided to begin by trying the asparagus, while also trying to figure out what Jasmin meant by heroes trying new things. However, when the food entered his mouth all thoughts of heroes and stories fled from his mind. For the next several minutes he focused completely on whatever was on the end of his fork or in his mouth.

Everything was delicious, and nothing was what he expected. Each dish had flavors he couldn't quite place but seemed to perfectly enhance the dish. Martin offered up a slice of duck, which turned out to contain a delicious balance of savory and sweet. Each bite was an exploration, a chance to discover anew how the flavors blended and complemented one another.

Finally, Martin spoke. "Are you ready now for the third story?"

Jeff nodded his head, still wanting to focus entirely on the food, but also too curious about the third story not to press on.

"The third story is the story you tell about yourself," said Martin. "It is the story you tell about what you can and cannot do. When Jasmin was in her old job, what stories was she telling about what she could do?"

Jeff thought about the way Jasmin had described her situation. "She seemed to feel stuck. She didn't have the energy to leave. She didn't have the mind-set to reach out to or connect with other people. She didn't seem as if she could do much of anything, at least nothing positive."

"And that's the story," Martin said triumphantly. "She was the perfect victim — helpless, vulnerable, weak. When we tell stories about ourselves, we frequently tell ourselves what we can't do. Jasmin told herself a bunch of these stories. She can't change her boss. There are no jobs out there, so why look? She was full of what she couldn't do."

"So what should she have done?" Jeff asked.

"She should have asked herself a new question. She should have asked, what would the hero do?"

> ## Self Stories
>
> Victims tell stories in which they are unable to change themselves or the world around them. Ask, **what would the hero do?** to discover the actions you can take.

"Before it was see, now it's do," said Jeff. "Does that mean it's finally time for action?"

"You bet. Think about your favorite books or movies. The heroes are almost always faced with a challenge that seems insurmountable. They are trapped with nowhere left to run, but they always seem to find a way. They find something they can do that turns their situation around. So the question that turns around the third story is, what would the hero do? Think about Jasmin's situation. What kinds of things would she have done if she were the hero in her story?"

Jeff imagined Jasmin's story as a movie. The young heroine pursues the job of her dreams. When she finally arrives on the scene of her fantasy, the reality is far from fantastic. Her boss is cruel, the restaurant is failing, and her hours are brutal. Then comes the turning point in the plot, and everything starts to improve.

Jeff smiled. "Now I can really see it as a movie. If Jasmin were the hero, she would have come up with ideas to save the restaurant. She might have confronted her boss about his behavior or suggested new recipes. She would have been lighthearted on her date and would have fallen in love. She would even have won over the other bitter employees and turned them into eager, motivated workers."

"That's pretty good," Martin laughed. "I think it's almost ready for the big screen."

"This makes sense to me. The hero doesn't just accept the situation. He takes action. He changes things."

"Or *she* takes action," chided Martin.

Now it was Jeff's turn to laugh. "That's right. After all, Jasmin is the hero here."

Then something else occurred to Jeff. He thought he had found a flaw yet again.

Walk Away

Some things in life are more complicated than the average movie script. Most real situations lack a Hollywood ending. These thoughts caused Jeff some concern as he debated the value of the third story—the story about oneself.

"You know," Jeff said, "it was fun to describe heroic acts, but not every situation has a simple solution. In the scenario I described—in which Jasmin saved the failing restaurant—everything fell in line, but what if the other people didn't cooperate with her heroism? What if her old boss shot her down and continued to berate her?"

Martin became even more excited as he answered Jeff's question. "That's an important point. Just because she sees like a hero, takes notice of her boss's pain, and acts like a hero doesn't mean he won't continue to act poorly. I'm sure you've known people who would be tough to turn around no matter how heroic you were."

Jeff thought again about the Fast Track program he was in when he first started at the company. During his assignments, most of the people he worked with were nice, good people, but one of them—his name was Patrick—gave Jeff a bad feeling right from the start.

Patrick was always angling to take credit for successes and trying to pin blame on others when something went wrong. He gossiped incessantly, and Jeff was pretty sure he had started a couple of false rumors about some of their colleagues.

He said to Martin, "I can think of someone I wouldn't even want to be a hero with. Forget about turning him around."

"OK, so I assume this person is really unpleasant."

"Definitely."

"So what do heroes do with those types?"

Jeff was puzzled. "I thought you said heroes figure out a way to turn people around, confront them, change their behavior, and make friends with them."

"That's one option, but it's not the only option. Heroes who recognize they are attached to someone they don't want to be attached to walk away."

This surprised Jeff. "That doesn't seem very heroic."

Martin shook his head. "But it is. Remember, you aren't being a superhero, just a hero. Not every problem has a perfect solution. Think about the movies again. In some movies the main character saves the day, but in others the story is about how the main character experiences some kind of personal growth. The triumph for the hero isn't fixing everything in the outside world. The triumph is about growing stronger as an individual. Jasmin could have tried to change things at her old job, and her boss might have continued to berate her. The hero at that point wouldn't have stuck around for more abuse. She would have walked off into the sunset, stronger for her experience and eager to start anew."

Jeff thought he understood. "In my case, I was thinking about a guy who really rubbed me the wrong way at my company. What you're saying is I don't have to make friends with him to be a hero. In fact, I can walk away from him."

"That's right. Of course, it isn't always that easy. If the guy is someone you work with, you might choose to get a new job. That takes time, and you have to figure out how to be a hero while you still work with him. If he's in your family, you may never be able to walk away. Then you have a lifetime of being heroic with someone you don't like."

Jeff thought Martin had just described his situation with half his family. His father-in-law had extreme political views that drove him crazy. His cousin was incredibly selfish. He'd tried to change both of them, but they were impossible. Now he tried to imagine how he could act like a hero with someone who drove him crazy.

He remembered that being a hero isn't always about saving or changing someone else. It can also be about experiencing personal growth. So he imagined how it would play out if this were a movie. He met and got to know his father-in-law. At first the two of them fought all the time, and the father-in-law never changed.

Jeff realized he couldn't adopt his father-in-law's political views — that wouldn't be heroic if he didn't believe in them. Then Jeff thought about how the hero has the strength to walk away from a bad situation. He imagined walking away without walking away.

There was a big family dinner with his father-in-law, as usual, talking about politics nonstop. Then the scene shifted from the norm. Instead of arguing with him, Jeff changed the conversation. He couldn't walk away from the relationship, but he could walk away from that discussion. He deftly changed the topic and then turned to speak with someone else. Just because his father-in-law said something he disagreed with, didn't mean Jeff had to argue the point. Being a hero usually meant fighting for what he believed in, but maybe it also meant knowing when not to fight.

Jeff described this scene to Martin, who nodded his head in agreement.

"So all I have to do is ask, what would the hero do?"

"That's it," Martin replied, "but don't forget the first two stories. First you have to see like a hero, then you can act like one."

The Hero's Ideas

Jeff thought about the doubts he had when he first met Martin earlier that day. He had been concerned that the stories about other people and his situation left him a helpless bystander. Now things seemed to be turning around.

He thought about the ways the first two stories gave him the positive energy to act like a hero. When he told his old stories, he was far more likely to sit back and do nothing, falling into patterns that made him angry and ineffective. When he told the new stories he had learned about this week, he was much better able to act in new, positive ways.

When Jasmin described how despondent she was in her old job and how she had acted out by sabotaging the cooking, Jeff had been a little shocked by her behavior. Now he realized he had his own confessions to make. He was embarrassed by some of the things he had done, but he wanted to learn how to turn his situation around. So he told Martin his story.

"My daughter cries almost all the time. That may not sound like a big deal, but it gets to you. The crying has been tough on me, but it has been worse on my wife. She takes it much harder than I do. Still, I dread going home sometimes. I'm ashamed to admit it, but I've stayed late at work a lot this year when I didn't have to. I've left my wife to do the work even though she probably feels more burdened than I do. That certainly doesn't feel very heroic."

Jeff glanced at Martin to see if he was shocked by this story. He was afraid Martin would think he was an awful person, but Martin just gave him a reassuring smile.

"None of us are heroes all the time, and you're just learning this."

"Still," Jeff said, "thinking back on my actions I feel terrible. I mean, I love my wife. I don't want to burden her, but that's exactly what I've done. She almost never calls me to say she'll be late coming home. She always takes the responsibility, and I've left her with it every time I pretend to work late."

Martin tried to reassure him. "It's a lot easier to know the right thing to do than it is to actually do it. Again, that's why the first two stories are so important. Take your situation as an example. Think about your old stories and how much your new stories will change the way you act."

Jeff considered this. His old stories were all about him. He had a tough kid who made him miserable. He got beat up by his boss all the time, and the last thing he wanted was to follow that by getting beat up by his kid. Plus, taking care of her usually led to a fight with his wife. Life was pretty awful.

With all of those stories he still knew the right thing to do was tell the truth and go home when he could. He knew that, but with his victim stories he didn't have the energy to care — at least not enough to act.

With his new stories he felt better. He was in touch with his daughter's pain and his wife's struggles. He wanted to help them. He felt for his boss, too, and wanted to help her. He no longer believed his life was awful; rather, it was challenging with many bright spots.

He described this to Martin and then asked, "What about the times when I feel overwhelmed or intimidated by my circumstances?"

"What do you think?" Martin asked in return. "Does that mean you aren't a hero?"

Jeff considered this for a moment. "I don't think so. Heroes are heroes because they stand up in the face of the challenge. You can feel afraid and still be a hero. You can even become overwhelmed sometimes. It's how you act despite your fear that makes you a hero. If I was the hero, I might still dread having to care for my crying daughter and my exhausted wife, but I would go home on time or early despite that feeling. It would even be exciting at times to take on the challenge, knowing I was doing the right thing."

Parable

Martin gave Jeff a big smile. "Go on. What else would the hero do?"

"I'd bring my wife little presents now and then for no reason. I'd look for ways to make her life better and also try to find ways we can both make things better for our daughter."

"Yes," Martin said. "You've got it. And what about your situation with your boss? What would the hero do there?"

"Two things come to mind," replied Jeff. "The hero would spend less time being angry with her and more time figuring out how to improve. Instead of figuring out how to be a star performer, I've rebelled against her lessons. I should try to anticipate her needs and change my own behavior before she has to say anything to me."

"Now you sound like a hero. What was the second idea?"

"This one is tough," Jeff said. "Even if I do better in my job, there will still be times when she or someone else treats me in a way I don't like. I think if I was a hero, I would be willing and able to speak my mind, to tell her how her actions have affected me."

"That is tough," Martin agreed. "Try to clarify it a little. How would the hero do that?"

"I'm not exactly sure, but I know how the hero wouldn't do it. He wouldn't go in guns blazing and blaming her for everything. The hero would strike a balance between accepting responsibility and describing the challenges caused by her actions."

"That's good," Martin said. "I also like to say the hero has ideas. You may not have the best solution, but you need to have a suggestion. The hero doesn't dump problems in someone else's lap without at least trying to find a solution."

"OK, so I need to have some ideas about how Yvette and I can work better together."

There was a pause in the conversation, and as the silence stretched out, Jeff knew Martin wasn't going to let him go on this point until he came up with an idea of his own. Jeff furrowed his brow. Then something came to him.

He used to think of Yvette as a teacher. He wanted to soak up the knowledge she had. Somewhere along the line he stopped seeing her as a teacher and started to see her as a judge. At the same time, deep down, he knew she wanted him to do well. She didn't want to pronounce him guilty.

"I think it would help," Jeff said, "if I felt I was expected to be learning, that some mistakes were OK. On the other hand, sometimes I know I will do things when I really should know better. If we could distinguish between learning moments and moments of judgment, it would help me understand where I stood. What do you think?"

"I think it's not up to me to judge your idea, but I will say this. You're always more of a hero when you walk in with an idea. So I'd say you're much better off now than you were before you came up with this one."

"You know, I feel better, too. Whether it's with my boss or my wife, I want to walk in with an idea. I want solutions — they make me feel better about myself and the possibilities in my situation."

Martin smiled at him. "You almost identified the third strength. When you ask yourself what the hero would do, you are building the strength of hope. When you believe you have no options, you are a victim. The victim is hopeless, but the hero is never hopeless. The hero always believes there is a way to make things better."

"You know," Jeff said, "I do feel hopeful."

> Heroic stories about yourself build hope.

The Ultimate Storyteller

The restaurant was still bustling when Jasmin walked up to Jeff and Martin's table with three plates in her hands. On each was a soufflé dish with a different-colored soufflé rising above the top.

Martin was smiling. "It looks like Jasmin has been busy since we last saw her."

"I hope you don't mind," she said. "I took the liberty of ordering dessert. Because you are a nut, my old friend, you get the hazelnut. Jeff, only the best for you — the Grand Marnier soufflé — because everything is better with Grand Marnier. And for me," Jasmin said, sitting down, "well, girls do love chocolate."

Once again Jeff forgot about stories while he lost himself in the flavors of his food. He had never experienced anything as light and smooth as this soufflé. The flavors were downright sensual. After a few minutes of gastronomic pleasure, Jasmin broke the silence.

"So, have you told him about Sal yet?"

Martin sighed. "You do have a way of letting the cat out of the bag."

"Sal?" asked Jeff. "You mean pizza Sal?"

With that Jasmin got up, winked at Jeff, and started to walk off toward the kitchen. Before she got too far away, Jeff called Jasmin's name.

She turned back and he said, "Thank you. Thank you for giving me hope." Jasmin smiled and then continued walking away.

They sat in silence for a minute, each experiencing his own feelings of respect for Jasmin. Eventually, Martin turned to Jeff with a grin. "She is something else."

Jeff smiled. "Yes, she is. Now what's this about Sal? Do I get to hear his story?"

Martin took a deep breath and stared into his empty soufflé

dish for a few moments. Then he said, "Actually, you've already heard his story. Sal is the man I met in a hospital cafeteria five years ago. He taught me how much I have in this life. Then his wife — her name is Rosalyn — taught me that even in the worst of times, some stories bring you farther down and others help lift you up. In different ways Sal taught me all three of the stories we have discussed. From the time I first met him all the way through to today, he has been the most inspiring person I've ever known."

Then Martin gazed up at the ceiling as though searching for some higher knowledge. "Some people in my company are a bit confused about the time you and I have spent this week. We have a lot going on as a company, and I've disappeared now for three large chunks of time."

Jeff felt guilty hearing this, but he didn't know what to say. As if Martin could read his mind, he said, "Don't worry. Spending this time was my choice. You didn't take this time from me — I gave it freely. The truth is Sal needs to be a hero this week. In some small way, carrying this message to you makes me feel I'm doing what he would do."

Jeff couldn't help noticing the emotion in this comment. He didn't want to intrude, but his curiosity got the best of him. "Why is that? What's happening this week?"

Martin looked across the restaurant for a long time. "Sal and his wife haven't stopped fighting for their son. For five years now they have looked for any solutions they could find, any possibilities that might give him a happier, less stressful life. Unfortunately, he still experiences seizures on a regular basis. They aren't as frequent or as debilitating as they once were, but they're not something you'd want to live with.

"This week they are starting him on a new set of somewhat experimental drug treatments. It's a very difficult time for the whole family. Rosalyn is staying with him full-time, but Sal still has his restaurant to run."

"Wow," Jeff replied. "On a positive note, I guess from what you said that his wife survived the breast cancer."

"She did. She came out stronger than ever and still telling amazing stories. Just this morning I spoke to her and Sal. I wanted to check in and wish them well. She told me they were doing fine. Then she told me how lucky they felt. She talked about how many people have supported them for these past five years, through three brain surgeries and her breast cancer. She described how uplifting that support has been. Their son will never fully develop. He has a lot of mental difficulties. So they've had a challenging time raising him. Instead of focusing on the difficulties, she is, as always, telling the story of her good fortune."

Jeff shook his head. "I think I can use these stories to deal with a crying baby, to make me a better husband, and to make me better at my job, but I don't know that I could do what you just described. They must be very special people."

"They certainly are," Martin agreed. "But there is something else to keep in mind. Telling stories is a skill. The more you do it, the better you will get. It may be tough for you at first to tell heroic stories, especially when you are stressed out or angry. Don't give up on the idea. Keep telling the stories. The more you do it, the more it becomes a natural part of the way you respond to tough situations. Sal and Rosalyn are very special. They've also been honing this skill for a long time."

"Don't worry about me practicing," Jeff replied. "Based on how this has helped me already, I'm ready to do whatever it takes to master my hero stories."

"In that case, I have a very important story to tell."

Jeff's eyes opened wide as he quickly asked, "What is it? Is there a fourth story?"

Martin responded, "It's the story of the hero coach who goes back to his office on a very full and happy stomach."

At that they both laughed.

When the bill had been paid and they were back outside, Jeff looked Martin in the eye and shook his hand. Once again he was struck by the power of Martin's stare. His eyes seemed to say he understood a great deal, and Jeff knew this to be true. They released hands and Martin hailed himself a cab.

The Mountaintop

One year later, it was hard for him to believe but Jeff was moving into a new job. Yvette had been true to her word. Within twenty-four months of going to work for her, he had been promoted.

As part of the new role, he was participating in his company's leadership development program. The first part of the program was a one-week intensive training experience at his company's headquarters in Zurich, Switzerland.

On the flight he reflected on how his new stories had changed his life over the past year. During the performance review he had dreaded so much, Yvette had delivered some strong messages. Without his new stories, he would have taken them as criticism and rebelled against them. His new stories allowed him to see her comments as recommendations that could help his career.

He had then worked with his team to shift their stories about other departments. Now they enjoyed stronger, more collaborative relationships all over the company and were consistently invited to partner on important projects.

He recalled when Yvette first offered him a job in her department. He had dreamed of having a team of people who would run through walls for him. As a manager, he had been good but not great at first. In the last year heroic stories had changed that. The stories his team now told had built up more camaraderie, team spirit, energy, and enthusiasm than anything else he had ever done as a manager.

Jeff knew his team supported him, and his heroic stories

helped him care more about them. His teammates were also a major reason his stories had shifted so effectively. He had taught them all about the lessons he learned from Martin. No sooner did he teach them than they began catching him in victim stories. They developed a rallying cry.

What's your story? was a question that flew around the team's office space. Anytime someone drifted into victim territory the team was ready to pull them back.

Then Jeff thought about his family. Siena was sleeping through the night. That had nothing to do with his stories, but the wonderful new development came with a surprise attached: his problems didn't disappear.

The sleep deprivation was so challenging he had always assumed once Siena started sleeping through the night, parenting would be easy. His relationship with Marie would be easy. Life would be easy. Unfortunately, none of that was the case.

Once Siena started sleeping through the night, all of Jeff's troubles didn't magically disappear with the wonder of eight hours of sleep each night. He discovered new parenting, marriage, and life challenges. Fortunately, Jeff was prepared to meet these new challenges with his new stories.

Martin had told Jeff that new stories would change his life, and he was right. Jeff was hard pressed to find any area of his life that hadn't improved as a result of the new stories he told.

Jeff arrived in Zurich and attended a leadership program that was fun, interesting, and intense. In the opening the instructor said, "Making you a better leader is great for this company, but it's even better for you personally. When you become a better leader, you become a better parent, a better spouse, and a better friend. In short, this week you will become a better person."

When the program was over Jeff thought the instructor was right. He did feel like a better person, and he wanted to get home to share the lessons he had learned with Marie. He even wanted to tell two-year-old Siena about some of them. However, before he went home he decided to spend a couple of extra days in Switzerland.

The train ride from Zurich to Interlaken was only two hours. Looking out the window during the trip, Jeff was once again awed by the scenery. As he had nearly ten years before, Jeff found the mountains breathtaking and inspiring.

The town was as he remembered it — a beautiful mountain village nestled among towering mountain peaks. The walk to the youth hostel was longer than he remembered, but when he arrived, it seemed very little had changed other than the styles the kids were wearing.

In the common room the bulletin board was still there and still filled with pictures. Across the room Jeff saw the Guru. His beard had grown longer, but otherwise he looked the same. Jeff sat down and waited patiently by the bulletin board. He wasn't sure how long he had been lost in his thoughts when the Guru sat down opposite him.

The Guru smiled and said, "You're back."

Jeff was more than a little surprised. "You remember me?"

"No, I don't remember you specifically, but I know you."

Jeff thought about this for a moment, then nodded his head. "I suppose you would. I imagine you've spoken to a lot of people like me."

"A few. I call you my Bavarian gentians."

"What's that?"

"The Bavarian gentian is one of the beautiful flowers of the Alps. It wants to peek through the ground when many other flowers are bursting onto the scene early in the season, but for some reason it waits. Then once the other flowers have had their moment, the gentian blooms late in the season. Although it may take longer to reveal itself, it is a beauty with true blue color.

"I can usually tell from the look of someone like you. You are a gentian. You've been here before, but you didn't find what

115

you were looking for. Now you've come back because you finally made your discovery."

Jeff nodded his head in agreement. "When I was here almost ten years ago, I thought being on top of the mountain meant always having great experiences. I wanted to live my life jumping from one great experience to the next, always on a mountaintop. Life isn't like that. There are a lot of great experiences and a lot of lousy experiences. Now I realize it is more about how you respond to each than it is about making every single one a peak experience."

The Guru smiled. "You've learned a lot."

"Ten years ago I noticed there were two kinds of pictures on the bulletin board, but I only paid attention to the ones with kids on mountaintops. I saw the ones that looked like me back then, young kids on adventures. I didn't pay any attention to all the other pictures."

At this Jeff looked over at the bulletin board. There were the pictures he mentioned of the young adults on mountaintops with their knowing looks. There were also many other pictures of older adults in various places — homes, offices, hospitals, along rivers, in fields. They, too, had the knowing look in their eyes, but they had slightly more maturity.

The Guru followed his gaze. "Not everyone learns the important lessons early in life. Lots of people ignore or miss the wisdom on the mountains. Then years later they discover what they need. They finally figure out how to live the life they desire. Some of them send me their pictures then."

Jeff pulled out a picture. "I took this a few months ago. The other person in the picture hasn't been here, but I hope you'll post the photo anyway."

He handed the picture to the Guru, who took a long look at it. Eventually he stood up. Jeff saw he had a smile on his face. The Guru patted Jeff on the shoulder, nodded to him, walked over to the bulletin board, and posted the picture. Then he walked over to a table where a young man was reading a guidebook, sat down, and began talking.

Jeff sat for a few minutes. Eventually he rose and walked to the bulletin board and looked at the picture the Guru had just posted. It showed an Italian restaurant. Standing alongside Jeff was a man in a chef's coat with the name Sal embroidered in blue.

Afterword:
Find Your Heroic
Inspiration

꩜

In the past decade I have coached and taught thousands of people who were facing challenges. They suffered from critical bosses, missed promotions, loveless marriages, abuse from their customers, personal and health tragedies, or frustrations with their kids, their employees, or their companies.

Some clients had allowed minor issues to get under their skin; others had felt unable to recover from major disappointments. Whether they were dealing with everyday events or major life challenges, the stories they told themselves influenced their ability to curb their negativity, adopt a more positive frame of mind, and respond effectively to their challenges.

I had been helping people change their stories for years when my second daughter, at the age of six months, appeared to have a seizure. Her eyes rolled back in her head, her body stiffened, and she was unresponsive for about fifteen seconds. My wife and I took her to the hospital immediately, where she exhibited the same symptoms in front of five neurologists who had all squeezed into the room to see. They confirmed our fears. It looked like a seizure to them.

For five days we lived in the pediatric neurological unit of the hospital. One test after another came back negative. In the end, our daughter proved the neurologists wrong. Her symptoms were a bit unusual but were the product of a severe case of reflux. Her stomach, not her brain, was bothering her.

That week was one of the worst times of our lives. Still, we were lucky. It's easy for us to see that now. After all, our daughter was fine. She received medicine for her stomach, and all was right in her world. After all was said and done, we could smile and laugh.

The family who shared our hospital room, and with whom we have kept in touch over the years since, have faced a much longer ordeal. Sal's story is theirs. Their son had severe seizures and has endured more drug therapies than anyone should rightly have to experience, especially a child. He had undergone two brain surgeries when his mom was diagnosed with breast cancer, and he underwent his third brain surgery during her chemo treatments.

It is hard to imagine telling oneself a positive story under those circumstances. Yet they have and they do. They are quick to point out how fortunate they are, directing attention to their great doctors, their extremely supportive friends and family, and their ability to endure and overcome. To this day, I find them among the most inspiring people I have ever known.

Over the years since we met, I have observed the stories they have told. I also have listened for more than a decade to the stories my clients have told. Finally, I have become a keen observer of the stories I tell myself.

In each case I have discovered a clear link between the stories we tell and our ability to adapt, feel happy, work effectively, and achieve success. When our stories are empathetic toward others, we act in more constructive ways. When our stories are appreciative of what we have, we are more resilient and energized. And when our stories are empowering, they lead us to action. In short, we lead ourselves to be either heroes or victims.

Resource
Guide

Overview of Book and Online Resources

You may have observed that just reading a book might not be enough to change thoughts and behaviors that are not working in your life, and now you are wondering how to apply the lessons you have read to your own life.

This section can help you take immediate actions to cement the lessons of the book and can also serve as an easy reference guide any time you want to refresh your knowledge. You may decide to try one or all of the steps suggested.

Additional resources, tips, tools, and support are available at the hero Web site:

www.be-the-hero.com
Access code: HEROSTORY

Go to the Web site now and use the access code to enter the area reserved for readers of this book. Many additional resources are already available, and this is where I will continue to post new tools as I build them, and where you can ask me questions and connect with other readers in the forum.

At the time of the printing of this book the Web site included:

Weekly reminders. Sign up to receive a weekly email with a brief tip or message to support you in telling heroic stories.

Forum. The Hall of Heroes is a place for us to meet virtually, share stories, ask questions, and be in the company of heroes.

Tip sheets for managers. These one-page tip sheets help managers address such challenges as hiring heroes, coaching victims, heroic meetings, and much more.

Reading recommendations. These books have influenced me over my lifetime and supported me as I wrote this book.

Lesson plans. These guidelines will help instructors use this book to teach courses on leadership and psychology.

Audios. Special messages from the author comment on various passages in the book.

Additional questions to build hero stories. These questions will help you dig deeper to uncover your heroic stories.

Additional uses for hero stories. The parable focuses almost entirely on ways an individual can use the stories to build happiness and success. This section shows how these principles can be applied to the following:

Team building
Building family relationships
Brainstorming
Problem solving
Self-evaluation

Here's an overview of the following pages of the resource guide:

Be Aware of Your Hero and Victim Stories. The tools in this section will help you remember key lessons without rereading the whole book and help you keep the goal of telling heroic stories top of mind.

Build a Community of Heroes Around You. This section will help you build a support group of heroic storytellers.

Take Actions to Encourage the Hero in You. It isn't easy to tell a heroic story in the midst of a challenge or crisis, but this section offers techniques to teach yourself to respond with heroic stories when you might not be thinking clearly.

Hero Tips for Managers. These tips can help you start to become a heroic manager, and additional management tips are available at www.be-the-hero.com.

First Steps to Take Today. This is my last encouragement as you begin your heroic journey today.

The resources are designed to offer many choices. If you are having trouble deciding where to begin, I suggest you experiment with two or three options, and return to the book or check the Web site after you have worked with those for a while.

If you decide to only do one thing, my favorite tool is the smart cards in the next section, Be Aware of Your Hero and Victim Stories.

Remember, you are already a skilled storyteller. Everyone is. Your stories are vivid, detailed, and convincing. They move you to emotions and actions. The question is, are your stories moving you to the emotions and actions you want?

Now you can be more than a skilled storyteller. You can master hero stories. When you do so, you will determine the content, mood, and direction of your stories. In addition to being vivid, detailed, and convincing, they will also be energizing, inspiring, and productive.

The transition to telling heroic stories will not be instantaneous. The skill takes time to build, but as you practice, it gets easier. You will find that frequent practice telling heroic stories will make a big difference in your life. Your relationships will improve. Your effectiveness in your job will increase. You will respect and like yourself more when you tell a heroic story.

Then one day you will discover that something just happened that used to really bother you, and this time it rolled off your back. You responded productively, and without thinking, you told a heroic story. You didn't hesitate. There was not even a flicker of frustration. You have mastered your stories.

There is a path to learning any skill. Many steps may be required, but the journey starts with just one. Use the following pages to find suggestions for ways to begin your new journey.

Recognize Your Stories

Learning to change your stories takes practice. When you are in an emotional state, whether you are angry, disappointed, stressed out, or excited, your mind will be predisposed to fall back into old patterns and forget to focus on what the hero would see and do. The following tools can help you incorporate hero stories into your daily life.

I hope you enjoyed reading the parable and might even choose to reread it. However, you shouldn't have to reread it every time you want to refresh your knowledge. The first tool, the quick cards, can help you recapture the lessons of the book. Each of the three quick cards — one for each of the three stories people tell — contains a summary of the major lessons of that story. They are positioned on facing pages for easier photocopying. The quick cards can help you review and thus maintain your understanding of the book.

As you learn new behaviors, it is wise to keep in mind the phrase "out of sight, out of mind." The second tool, the smart card, can keep the lessons in view. I call them smart cards because they raise your storytelling IQ. These cards are the size of a business card, and they are meant to be used as visual reminders. Carry them with you. Post them on your desk, computer monitor, refrigerator, bathroom mirror, or dashboard. Put them anywhere you will see them and read them at least once a day.

Smart cards will keep your intentions about your new stories fresh in your mind. The more you can stay mindful of your storytelling, the more quickly you will learn to tell the stories you want to tell.

I encourage you to cut out or photocopy the following pages that contain the quick cards. The smart cards are on a perforated page at the end of the book. Don't leave them in the book on your shelf. Bring these cards into your life to help you tell your new stories.

Build a Community of Heroes Around You

One great way to cement your learning is to build a community of people who share the lessons and point of view. If your colleagues, family, or friends also understand the idea of storytelling, then the ideas from this book can become part of your common language.

You can help one another craft new stories when one of you is struggling. What story are you telling? can become a question you ask each other. You can hold one another accountable to keep using these techniques.

There are two great ways to build a community of supporters. The first is admittedly self-serving on my part. You could buy copies of this book for the people with whom you want to share this concept. The common grounding of Jeff's story and the smart cards can guide you as you help one another tell hero stories.

The second way is based on the truism "If you want to truly understand a subject, teach it." Get your group of supporters together and teach them about the three stories and how to turn stories around. Go to www.be-the-hero.com for more resources, including additional uses for hero stories and lesson plans for teaching this material.

With either of these two approaches, I recommend you gather with your group every couple of weeks or at least once a month to discuss the stories you have been telling. Share the stories you had to change and the new stories you told.

The more you share with one another, the more these techniques will become ingrained within you. After a while, telling new positive stories will be as habitual as the old negative stories were before you read this book.

Quick Card for People Stories

When You Are a Victim in Your People Stories

Foundation. Victim stories begin by making other people out to be mean, inconsiderate, or jerks. They ascribe motives to people that are unknowable. Victim stories are as likely to be false as they are to be true.

Short-term impact. The story that someone is being a jerk to you makes you angry and resentful. This makes you less happy and less able to perform effectively, whether on the job or at home. Your frustration with one person can spill over and affect how you interact with everyone else with whom you come in contact.

Long-term impact. If you consistently tell yourself the story that certain people (for example, customers, management, in-laws) are jerks, you will stop caring about those groups altogether. This will make you bitter and ineffective.

Shift to a Hero Story

Recognition. What story made you upset? Recognize the story you are already telling and the impact it has.

Question. Ask yourself the following question to see other people's challenges and shift your story:

What would the hero do?

Outcomes of Telling Hero Stories About People

Personal value. When you respond to someone else's pain, you feel concern for them and feel better about yourself.

Reciprocation. Being calm and caring will make others feel better about you. They will be more likely to be considerate of you in return.

Strength. Telling the story of someone else's pain builds the personal strength of *EMPATHY*.

Quick Card for People Stories

Facts About Hero Stories

Truth. Tell the story that makes you happier and more effective. The story that someone is in pain is no more likely to be true or false than the story that someone is a jerk. Since both are equally likely to be true, tell the story that leads to the emotions and actions you desire.

Squeaky wheel. People who are squeaky wheels shouldn't automatically get what they want. Seeing someone else's pain does not mean that you must help them. It does make you calmer and better able to make a clear and reasoned choice about what you will do for them.

Villains. Telling a heroic story brings you together with other people. People are rarely the villains in their own stories. If they are the villain in your story, you are almost certainly telling different stories. Such differences make it difficult for people to understand one another, which is part of the benefit of changing your story.

The pull. Recognizing that your old stories are enticing can help you to let them go. You may want to hold onto the story that reinforces what you've already decided. Don't get sucked in by the routine of your old stories.

Emotional shift. Changing your story will change your emotions. You can't stop being upset if your story makes you feel upset. You have to change your story, which will in turn change your emotions.

Quick Card for Situation Stories

When You Are a Victim in Your Situation Stories

Foundation. Victim stories begin when you make your life out to be difficult and disappointing. They are frequently based on envy of others and frustration over what you don't have.

Types. People tell two types of victim situation stories. Outward stories focus on others who have more than you do. Inward stories focus on the worst aspects of your life and neglect the best.

Impact. The story that your situation isn't what it should be makes you frustrated and bitter. Over time, such stories sap your energy and make you pessimistic about the future and fearful of changes in your world.

Shift to a Hero Story

Recognition. What story made you upset? Recognize the story you are already telling and the impact it has.

Question. Ask yourself the following question to recognize where you are looking and to shift your story:

What would the hero do?

Outcomes of Telling Hero Stories About Situations

Energy. When you see the best aspects of your life, you become energized. This energy gives you the strength to be happy and to act to improve your situation.

Community. When you have a positive view of your life, you will influence others to think more positively and will attract people with similar views. This makes it easier to maintain a positive point of view.

Strength. Telling the story of the best parts of your life builds the personal strength of *GRATITUDE.*

Quick Card for Situation Stories

Facts About Hero Stories

Truth. Focus on the truth that helps. The story that your situation is frustrating may be true, but there is very likely an equally true story that describes your situation in a more positive light. The object isn't to ignore difficulties in your life. Rather, it is to embrace the most positive elements in order to give you the energy to act.

Choice. You can always choose what to see. No matter what challenges you face, your story about your situation is based on where you choose to focus your attention.

Specifics. Find specific points of comparison that help you appreciate what you have. Starving people on the other side of the planet may not be as meaningful as a homeless person you pass on the street every day. And that homeless person won't be as meaningful as the one you meet and speak to when you volunteer at a soup kitchen.

Rights. You have every right to feel angry or sad, but you also have the right to feel grateful and happy. You have the right to feel anything you want. The question is, how is your anger or your sadness working for you? Does it lead you to outcomes that you desire? You will undoubtedly encounter situations in your life that disturb you. Now you know that you don't have to stay upset.

Quick Card for Self Stories

When You Are a Victim in Your Self Stories

Foundation. Your victim stories about yourself tell you that you have no control. These stories tell you what you cannot do. Whatever is happening is beyond your ability to influence, so you just have to sit back and endure.

Impact. The stories that things are beyond your control leave you feeling helpless. They take away your ability to take actions that might improve your situation. Over time, these stories can destroy your self-esteem and steal your dreams for the future.

Shift to a Hero Story

Recognition. What story made you upset? Recognize the story you are already telling and the impact it has.

Question. Ask yourself the following question to see what is possible and shift your story:

What would the hero do?

Outcomes of Telling Hero Stories About Yourself

Success. The hero takes action to create success. When you are the hero, you don't just accept the situation. You take action to change things. This is the fundamental attribute of the hero.

Strength. Telling the story of what is possible and what you are capable of builds the personal strength of *HOPE*.

Quick Card for Self Stories

Facts About Hero Stories

Strength. It takes strength to act like a hero. Therefore, the success of the hero story about yourself rests on the success of the prior two stories. Hero stories about other people and your situation give you the energy, power, and resourcefulness to tell a hero story about yourself.

Possibility. The hero sees options no matter what the challenge. Everyone experiences challenges that seem insurmountable. Heroes find some action they can take to turn their situation around.

Plot twist. In self stories, the hero figures out a way to create a turning point. Most stories include some struggle. What makes a story a drama instead of a tragedy is that there is a turning point. Without this element, the characters spiral deeper and deeper into despair. However, when the turning point occurs, everything starts to improve.

Self-change. In some cases the heroic action is to change yourself. However, some people and situations are beyond even the hero's ability to change. In those cases, the hero knows to let go and walk away. Sometimes this means actually leaving the people or situation. At other times this means letting go of personal needs or wants in order to create a more peaceful outcome.

Take Actions to Encourage the Hero in You

Sometimes, despite our best intentions, we get caught up in the moment and forget or find ourselves unable to make the changes we desire. Often people believe their failure is caused by lack of willpower: they just didn't have enough determination to do the right thing. I don't believe willpower is the key.

Rather, I believe we change by practicing new behaviors in a disciplined way. Regular practice will build your strength and make telling your new stories easier and more natural, even when you face a challenge. You can find many ways to practice the new pattern you want to establish. Try the following five suggestions or let them spark your own ideas for specific actions to guide you to new behaviors.

Keep a Story Journal

Take five minutes each day to write down the stories you tell in a small notebook. Record the victim stories that came to you, and then add the hero stories you told to replace the victim stories. If you didn't think of a hero story when your victim story arose, create one for your journal. You may be too late to change the situation that formed the victim story, but creating the hero story will help you build the skill for the future.

Create and Use a Mantra

A mantra is a sentence or phrase you say to yourself that helps you enter a positive frame of mind. You are then empowered to do what you want to do. Whenever you feel a victim story is seizing control of your thoughts and emotions, repeat your mantra to remind yourself to create a hero story. A mantra can be a great tool to calm you down and prepare your mind to think differently. Some mantras my coaching clients have used include:
- Assume best intentions.
- What's your story?

- Be the book.
- I am William Shakespeare.

As you can see, your mantra can be serious or silly, as long as it helps direct you to the new story you want to tell.

Phone a Friend

Many people believe venting is important. This can be true, but not when venting reinforces your negative beliefs and does nothing to turn them around. If you feel stuck in a victim story, talk to someone who understands the idea of storytelling. Ask them to help you craft a hero story. Working with a friend or a coach is a terrific way to extend the value of the community discussed in the section Build a Community of Heroes Around You.

Read Your Smart Cards

Some of my coaching clients carry their smart cards with them in their wallets or purses. When they find themselves facing a challenge, they pull out their smart cards for direction. They find this easier than trying to remember the lessons in a moment of crisis. With their smart cards handy, all they have to remember is to read the card.

Call a Time-Out

It's important to recognize when you can no longer think clearly. One of the best parenting ideas I've ever heard is for parents to give themselves a time-out when they are growing angry or frustrated. Sometimes you will be too worked up to tell yourself a new story. When that happens, call a time-out. Go for a walk or to your room. Take some deep breaths. When you have calmed down a little, then it is time to work on your hero story. The time-out can help you create the frame of mind you need to tell the story you want to tell.

Hero Tips for Managers

Managers can find many ways to apply the lessons of this book to become stronger, more effective leaders. I encourage you to go to www.be-the-hero.com to find additional tips and tools to become heroic leaders (access code: HEROSTORY). But here is your first tip sheet — five easy steps to creating a team of heroes:

• *Be the hero.* You are a role model and must lead by example. The strongest influence on your team's behavior is your own behavior. Tell yourself heroic stories and show your team you are choosing a positive outlook and seeking solutions.

Share your stories. When you have a positive interpretation of the actions of team members, other departments, customers, or senior management, share these stories. By doing so, you will help team members build their own stockpile of positive views.

• *Hear and shift.* When team members tell victim stories, it is important you recognize their concern, showing that you understand their perspective. Don't be critical of them for expressing their view. However, don't allow them to accept their own view as the only possibility. You might respond, "I understand why you might feel that way. How else could we view this situation?" Then explore heroic alternatives.

• *Reward heroes.* Recognize and reward the people on the team who act heroically. Catch people in heroic moments — telling positive stories, showing resilience, or taking action in tough situations. Encourage this behavior when you see it and express appreciation during team meetings to show everyone that heroic behavior is valued.

• *Make it a team effort.* Explain to your team what it means to be an everyday hero and ask them to help you and one another think and act like heroes. Ask for their suggestions for helping each other. Encourage members to support each other when you are not around, and create a rallying cry to keep everyone focused on being a team of heroes.

First Steps to Take Today

Now it is time for you to go and tell heroic stories and take heroic actions. If you have read this far, you have probably already recognized times in your life when you have been both a hero and a victim. As you work to become a master of heroic stories, take these three steps to move forward now:

Place your smart cards where you will see them regularly, and read them at least once a day, every day, for the next month. Awareness is the first step toward any change.

Tell someone else about these techniques. The best way to learn is to share your knowledge.

Go to www.be-the-hero.com and enter the access code HEROSTORY to find many additional tips and tools to help you think and act like a hero every day.

Remember, mastering your stories doesn't happen automatically. Just as it takes time and practice to learn how to play the piano, swing a golf club, or cook a perfect Grand Marnier soufflé, it also takes time to master your heroic stories. And even the world's best chefs still botch a dish every now and then.

Don't give up. Keep practicing. Never stop. Be the hero—your happiness and success depend on it.

Acknowledgments

Thank you to the heroes in my life who helped make this book a reality.

First, thank you to the entire Morgan-Schupler family, RJ, Kirsten, Kelsey, Brittany, Liz, and Rob, for your incredible actions over the past few years. Thank you so much for all you have taught me and for allowing me to share your story. And a special thank you to Big Will for your unyielding courage and determination. Always keep smiling.

Thank you to my mom and dad, who through both words and deeds taught me my earliest and strongest lessons about heroism.

To Liliane and Claude, you are such warm, positive, quiet, and unassuming people it is easy to forget all you have endured in life. I thank you for being a living example of the empathy and courage of a hero.

To my siblings, Deborah and Daniel, who once again were among those brave souls who read the first draft and made it immeasurably better.

To my editor, Johanna Vondeling, I am humbled to have someone of your talent, patience, daring, and honesty as a partner. To everyone at Berrett-Koehler, I hope you never grow tired of your authors claiming you are by far the best publishing house in the industry. Thank you for all you stand for and do.

To Joseph James Chung for building so much more than a Web site to support this book. To Sandra Craig and Detta Penna for making me sound more learned than I am. To Clive Jacobson for your subtle yet sophisticated cover design.

To the many, many readers and supporters who provided feedback and guidance, including Howard Behar, Peter Bregman, Carl Brody, Pat Buhler, Marilyn Bushey, Sid Chapon, Gail Cortese, Kevin Cuthbert, John Egbert, Mike Futterman, Andrea Goeglein, Frank Horowitz, Mike Jaffe, Meg Karakekes, Daniel and Pamela Landau, Stewart Levine, Suzanne Levy, Merry Marcus, Al Martella, Chris Morris, Judson Potter, Carolyn Rabin, Lauren Riggs, Jeff Rohwer, Janice Rutledge, Candace Sinclair, Karlin Sloan, Scott Stoogenke, and Graham Vandergrift.

To Marshall Goldsmith, for taking the time to support this book and for all of the inspiration you have given me over the years.

To Sharon Jordan-Evans, for your support and wisdom — I have been honored to have you as my champion and thought partner throughout this process.

To Joe and Deb Cupani and Darlene Scarangella, for taking the time, drinking some wine, and giving up your weekends to share your insights. To Marc Ferris, for support and suggestions, of which I'm sure I've only seen the tip of the iceberg.

To Dr. Alan "Moonlight" Graham, for once again helping me connect ideas to theory and vice versa.

To Jen Gould, for working tirelessly, believing relentlessly, and doing all the little things.

To the New York authors group — Leslie Yerkes, Mark Levy, Carol Metzker, and Sally Helgesen — for always helping me to think and see more clearly and better understand the world of publishing.

Finally, my greatest thanks will always be reserved for the three who recharge, challenge, and enrich me on a daily basis. You push me, believe in me, support me, and make me laugh. You are my inspiration. You are my heroes. To Beatrice, Sophie, and Ella, thank you.

Index

accountability, accepting, 3–4
actions
    reinforcing heroic behavior, 134
    responding with hero stories, 124
    stories that result in the desired, 129
    taking more positive, 102, 106
adversity
    responding positively to, 4
    stories of good fortune in the face of, 112
alternatives, finding heroic, 136
anger
    controlling your, 36–37
    effect on job performance, 41–42
    stories that result in, 42–43
appraisal
    completing the personal performance, 61–62
    writing a personal performance, 31, 57–58
Art
    lifetime of overcoming challenges, 10
    living on the beach, 86–87
asparagus, Jasmin's story about her first job, 97
attention
    focusing on the heroic, 131
    focusing on the negatives and ignoring the positives, 80–81

attitudes
    effect of circumstances on personal, 85
    hero vs. victim, 43–44, 82–83
    maintaining a positive, 69
    remaining calm under stress, 47
    your stories influence your, 2
audios, available on www.be-the-hero.com, 124
awareness
    of hero and victim stories, 124
    smart cards, 137

babies, parental lifestyle changes, 24–25
balance, recognizing both sides of a story, 81
Bavarian gentians, the Guru's, 115–116
behavior
    actions that reinforce heroic, 134–136
    be the hero, 136
    rewarding dysfunctional, ix
    sustaining altered, 4–5
behaviors, being a jerk, 39–44
birthplace, appreciating the value of your, 84
blind date, self-sabotage on a, 99–100

Index

Index

About the Author

Noah Blumenthal is president of Leading Principles, Inc., a coaching company that supports managers, executives, and CEOs in finding fresh perspectives and building heroic leadership for themselves and their organizations. As a keynote speaker, coach, and consultant, Noah has worked with Fortune 500 and Global 500 clients in financial services, hospitality, advertising, media, pharmaceuticals, consumer products, insurance, chemicals, industrial products, energy, and professional services. Noah's honors include being named by *Leadership Excellence* magazine as one of the world's "Top 100 Minds in Personal Development."

Noah has been featured in various media outlets, including *The New York Times*, CBS News, MSNBC News, the *Chicago Sun-Times, Investors Business Daily,* and *Newsday*, and his writings have appeared in the publications of the American Management Association and the Organizational Development Network. His two books, *Be the Hero* and *You're Addicted to You*, help readers develop personal accountability and self-leadership.

Be the hero!

Invite Noah Blumenthal to keynote your next meeting or conference and develop heroes in your organization.

Noah delivers entertaining, dynamic keynote addresses and highly interactive workshops, helping participants to find their own storytelling voices. For more information about these or other keynotes and workshops Noah delivers, please visit www.leadingprinciples.com or email info@leadingprinciples.com.

Another Book by Noah Blumenthal

You're Addicted to You
Why It's So Hard to Change—and What You Can Do About It

We all have things about ourselves we'd like to change. You probably believe that your success depends on your conviction. But willpower alone isn't enough because each of us becomes so thoroughly conditioned to act in old, counterproductive ways that negative behaviors become part of our very being. In a very real sense we become addicted to ourselves. The problem isn't that you aren't trying hard enough but that you've never learned the right way to make difficult changes. Noah Blumenthal details a proven three-stage strategy—illuminated with practical tools, techniques, and exercises—for breaking self-addictions and conquering damaging behaviors like anger, workaholism, risk aversion, procrastination, overeating, underexercising—just about anything.

Paperback, 184 pages, ISBN 978-1-57675-427-6
PDF ebook, ISBN 978-1-57675-525-9

BK° Berrett–Koehler Publishers, Inc.
San Francisco, *www.bkconnection.com*   800.929.2929

Berrett–Koehler
BK Publishers